Frances Tosdevin & Jen Khatun

Farid's First Day

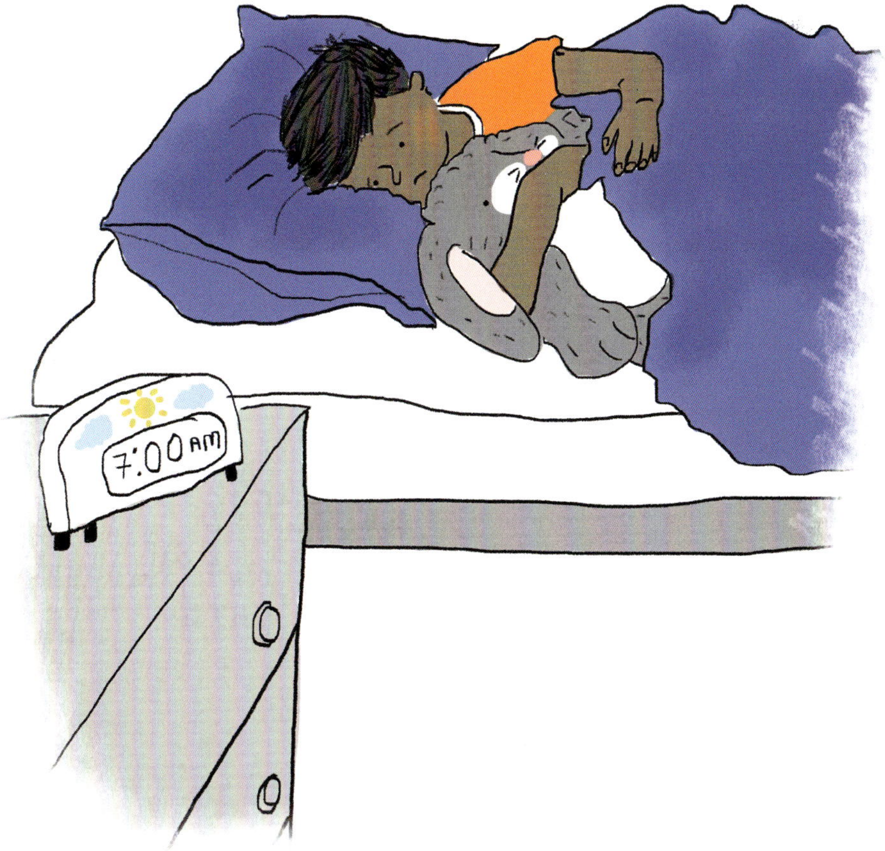

Collins

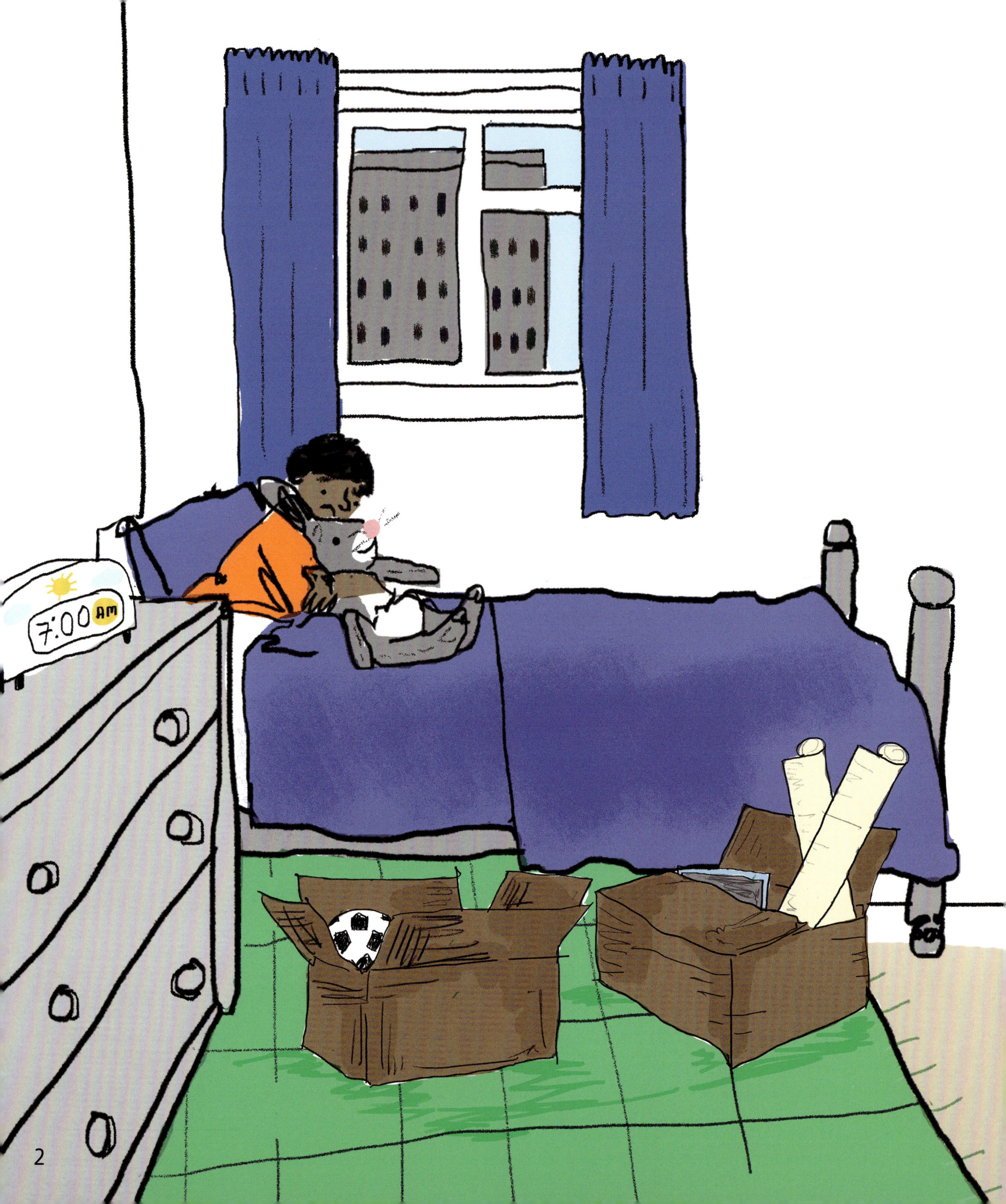
7:00 AM

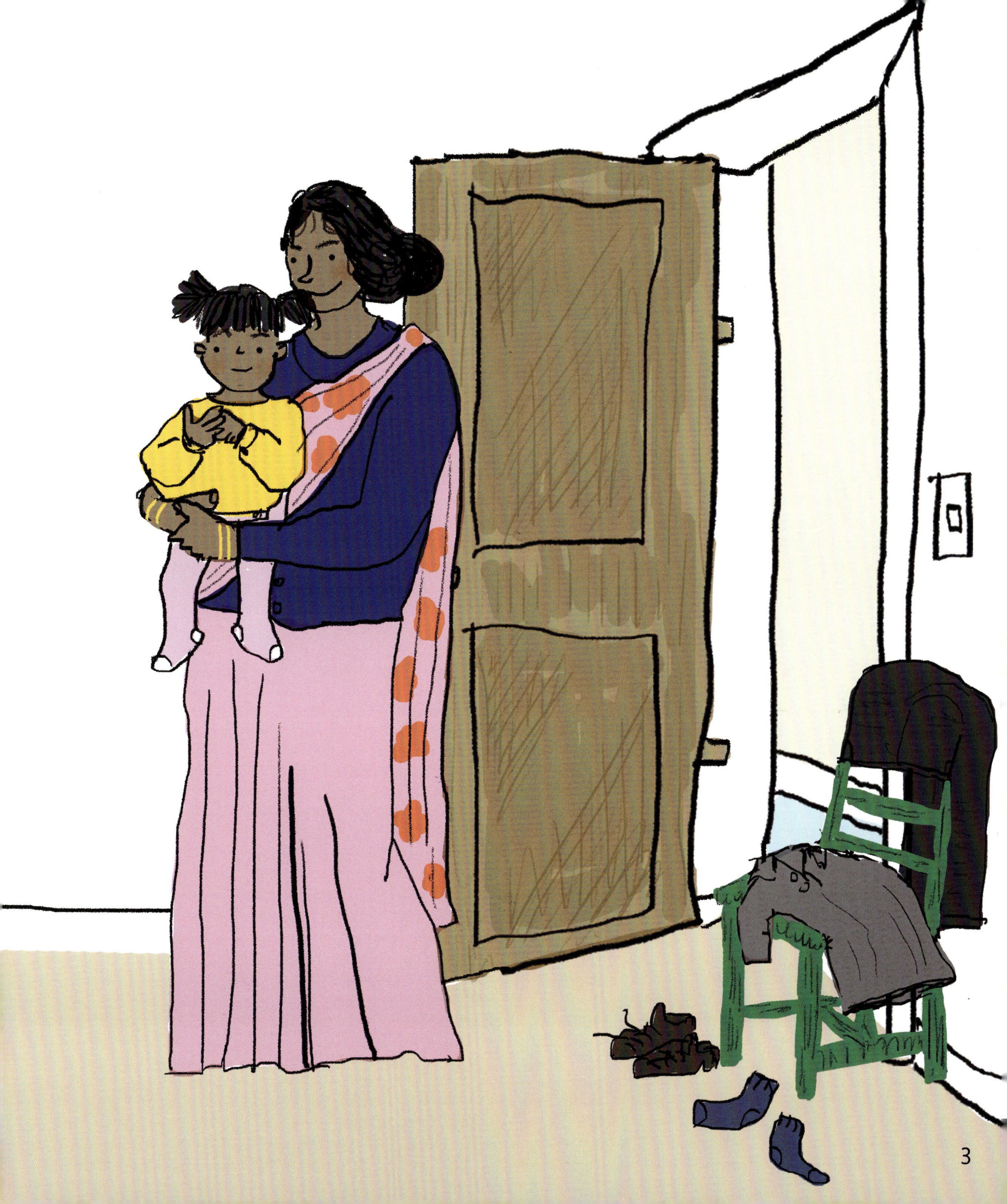

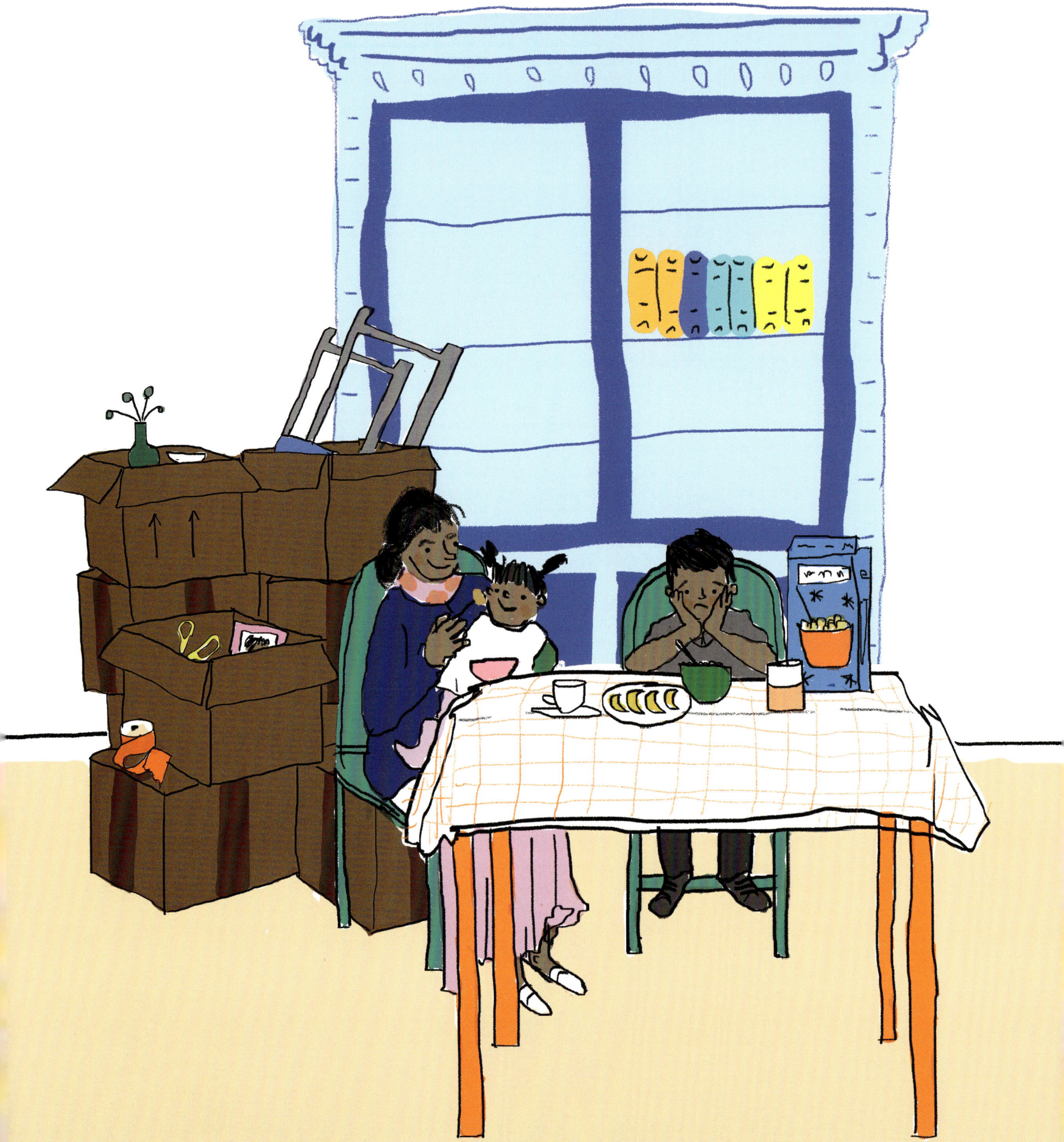

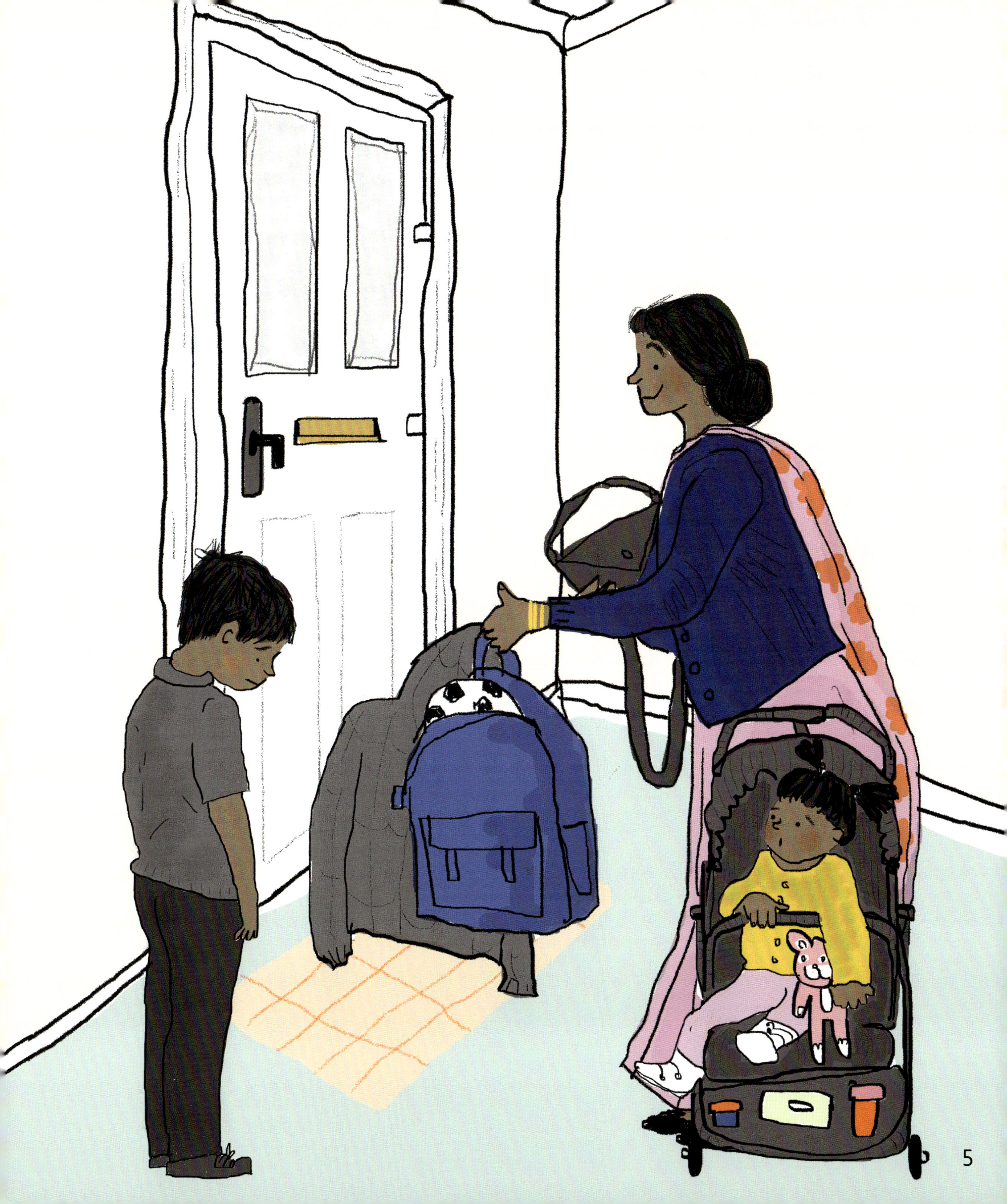

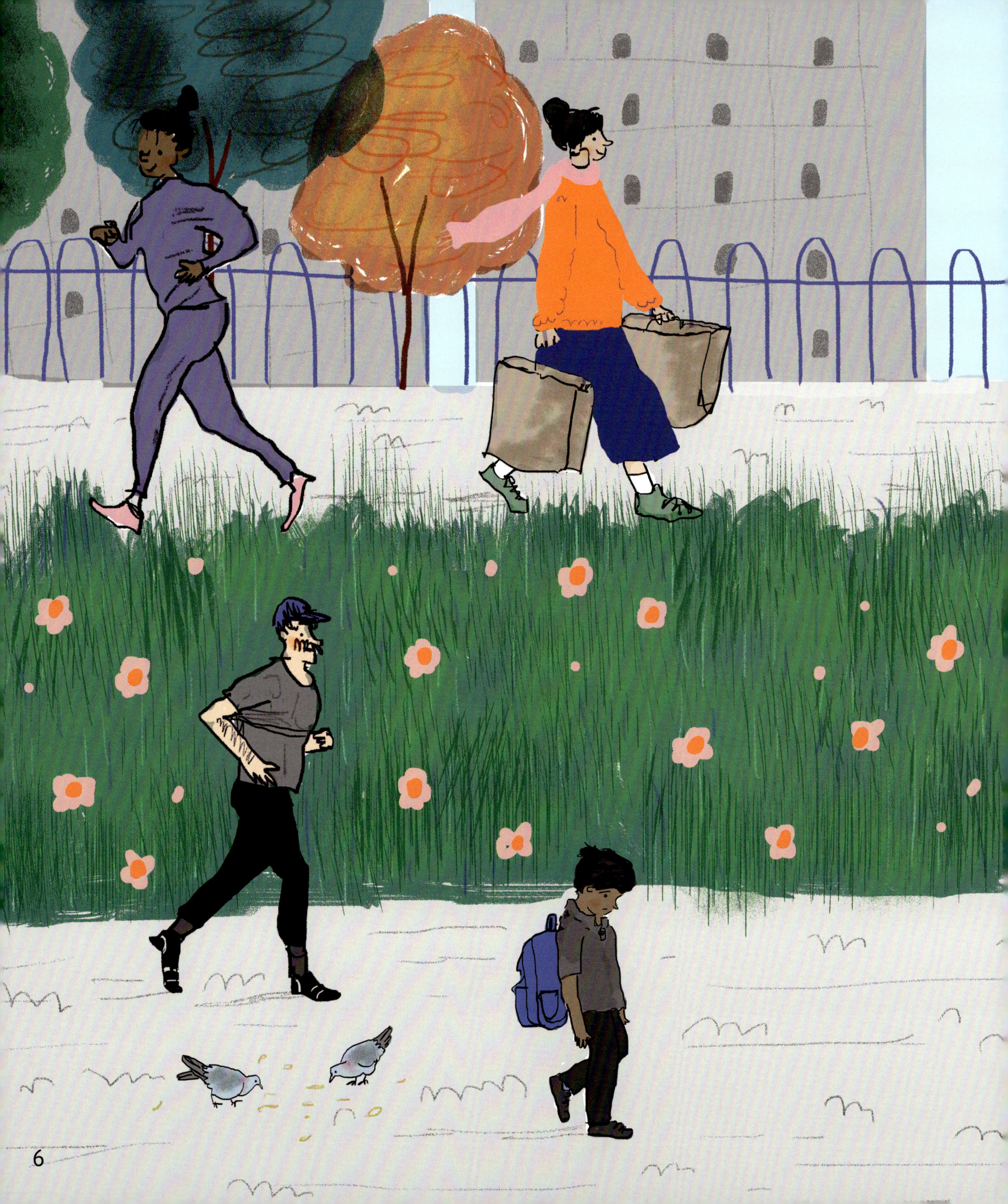

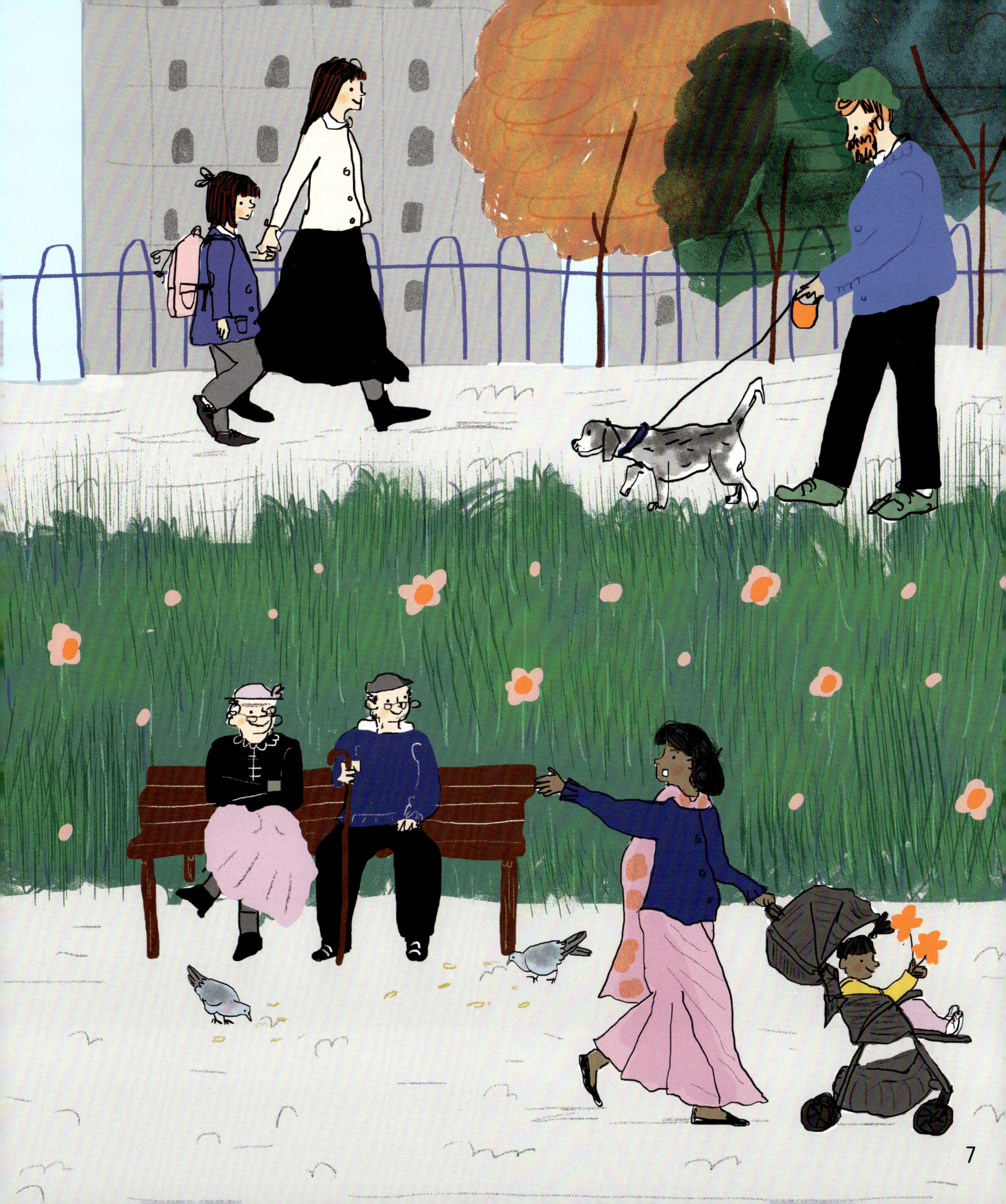

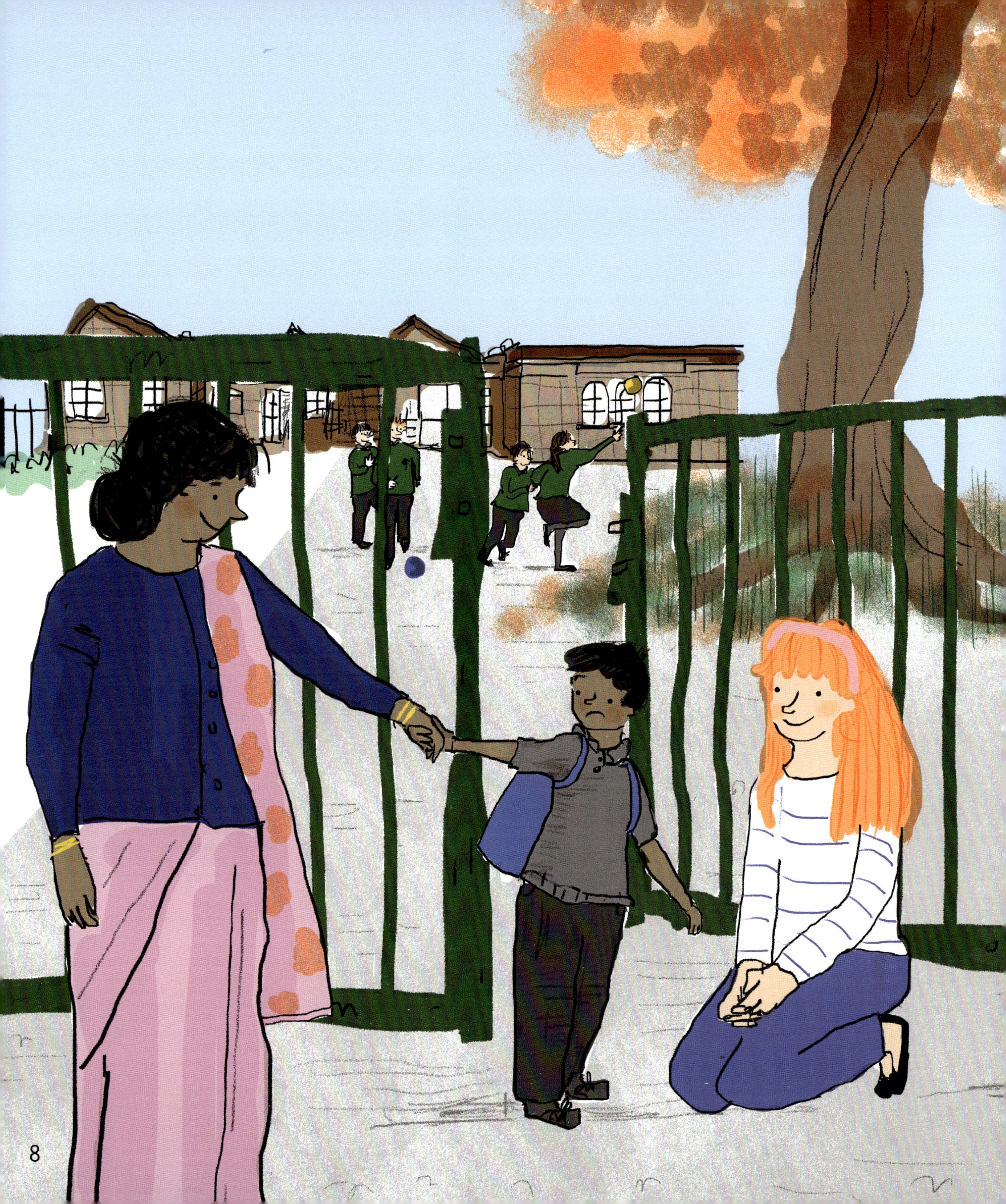

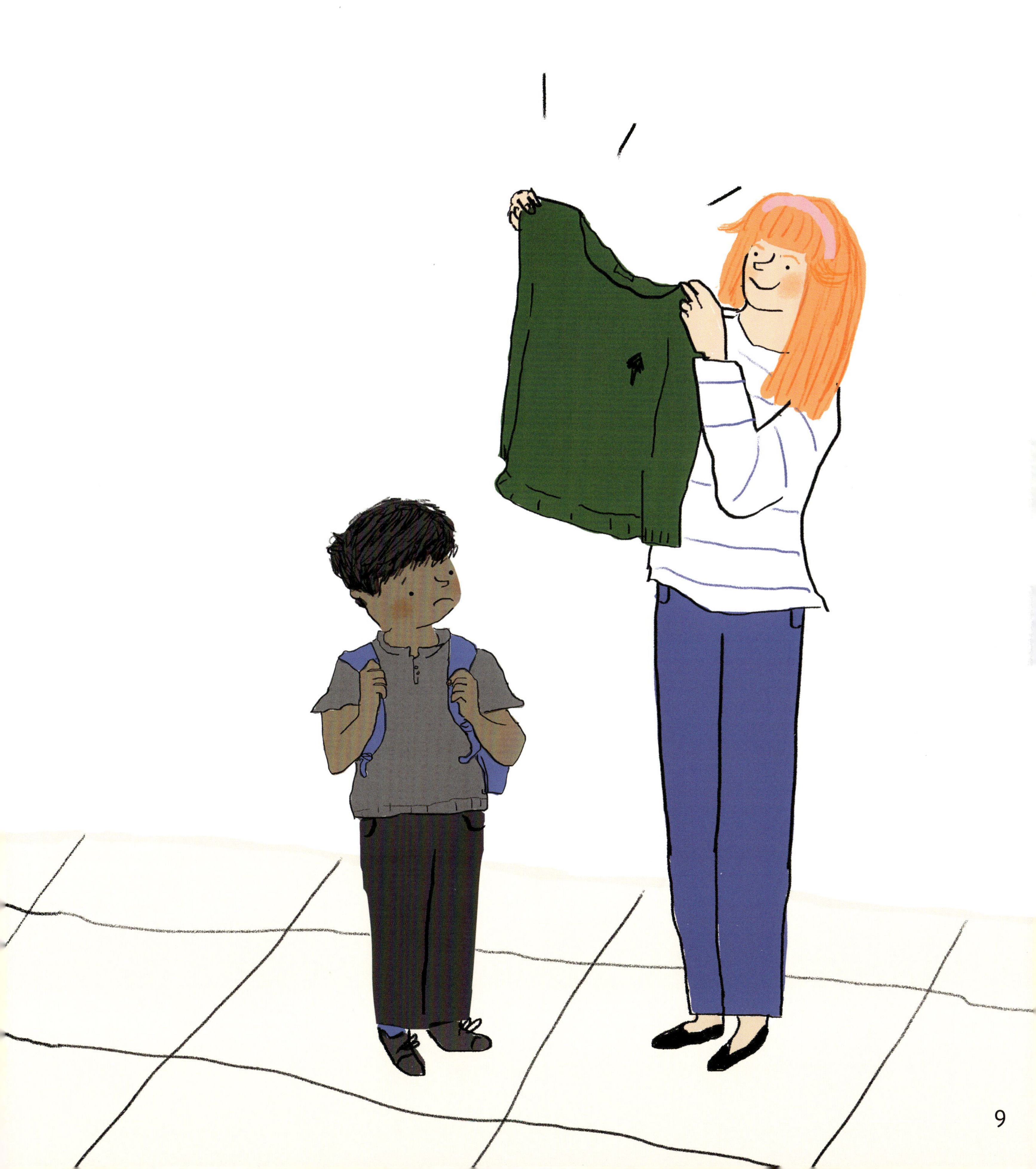

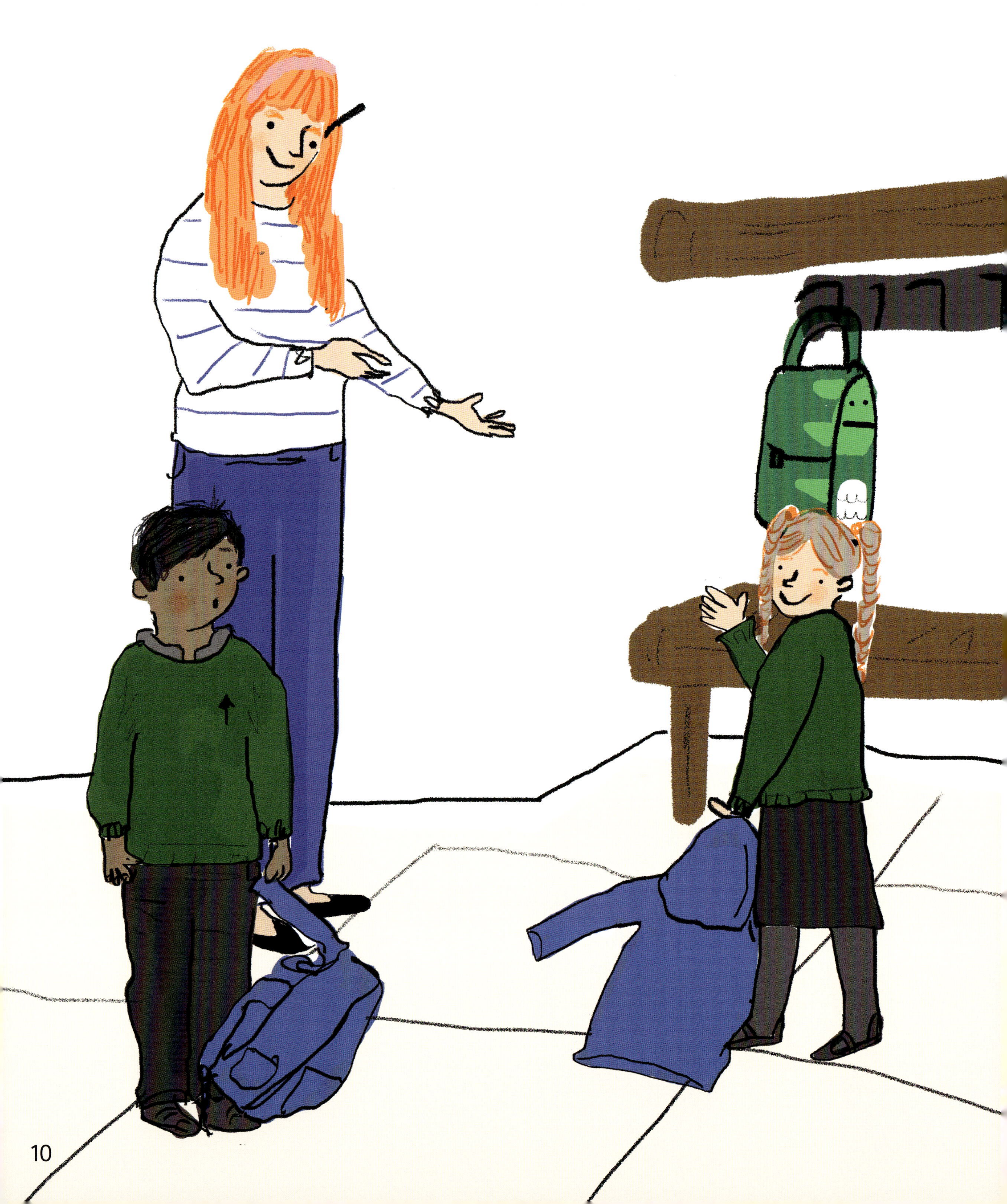

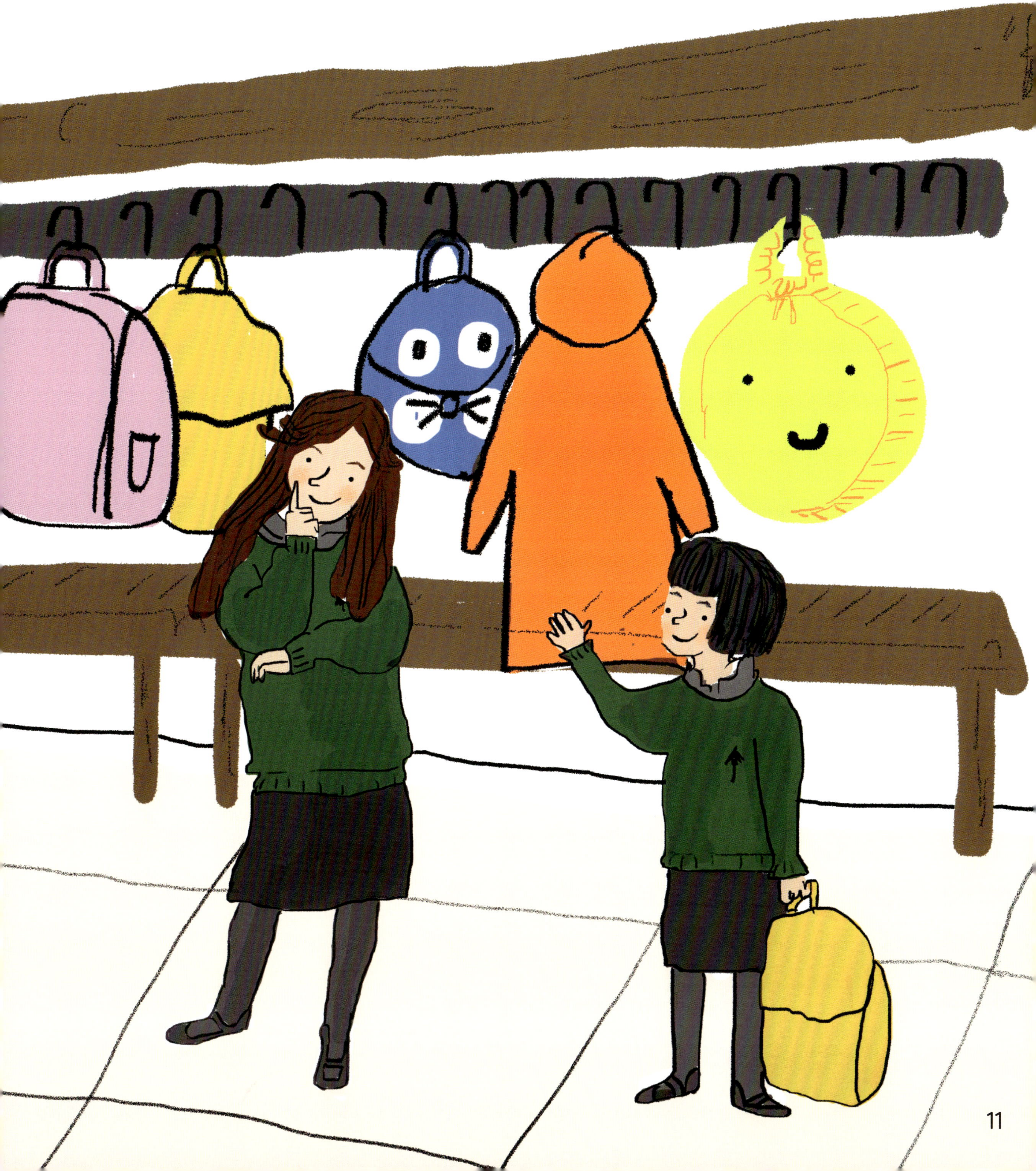

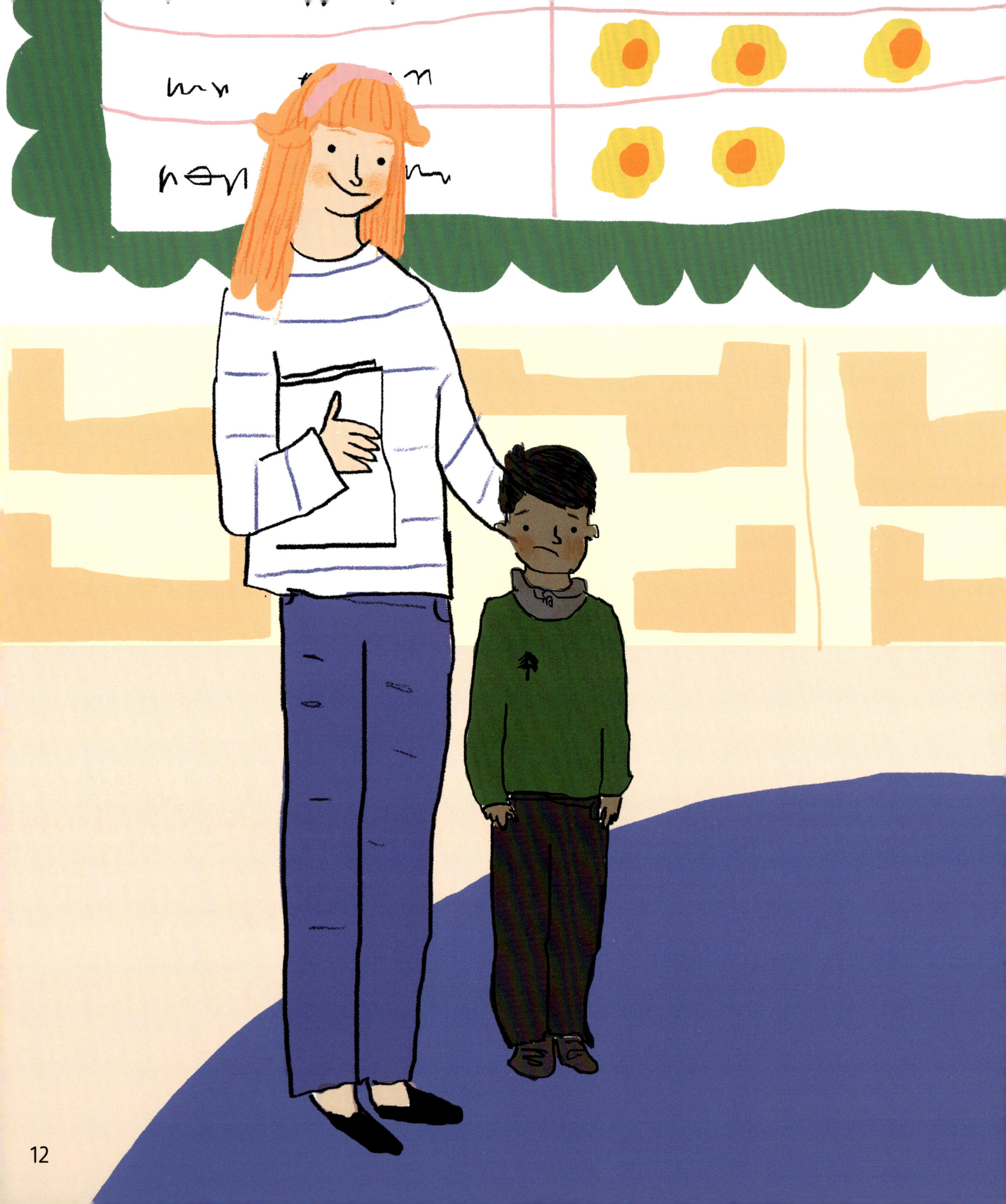

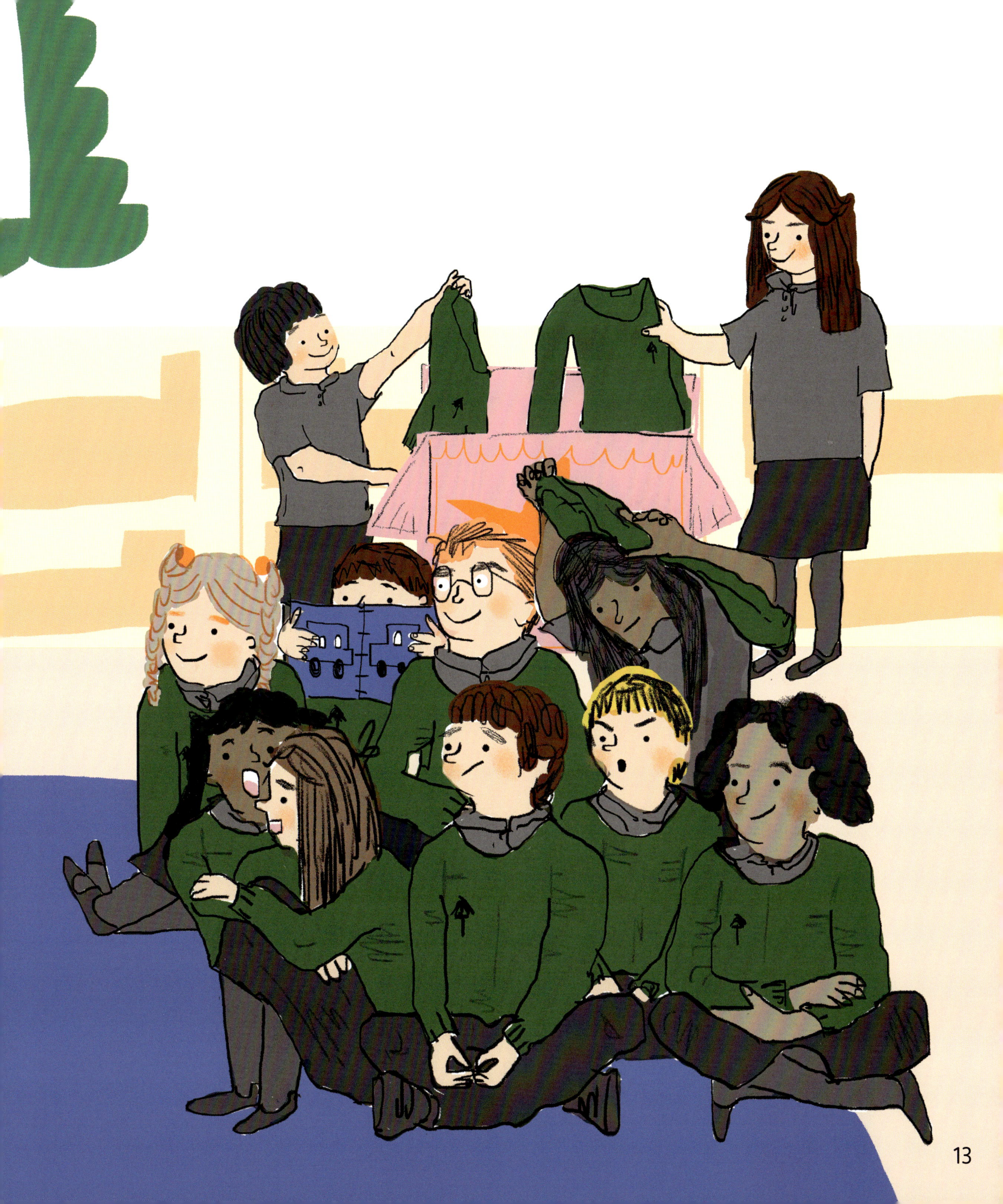

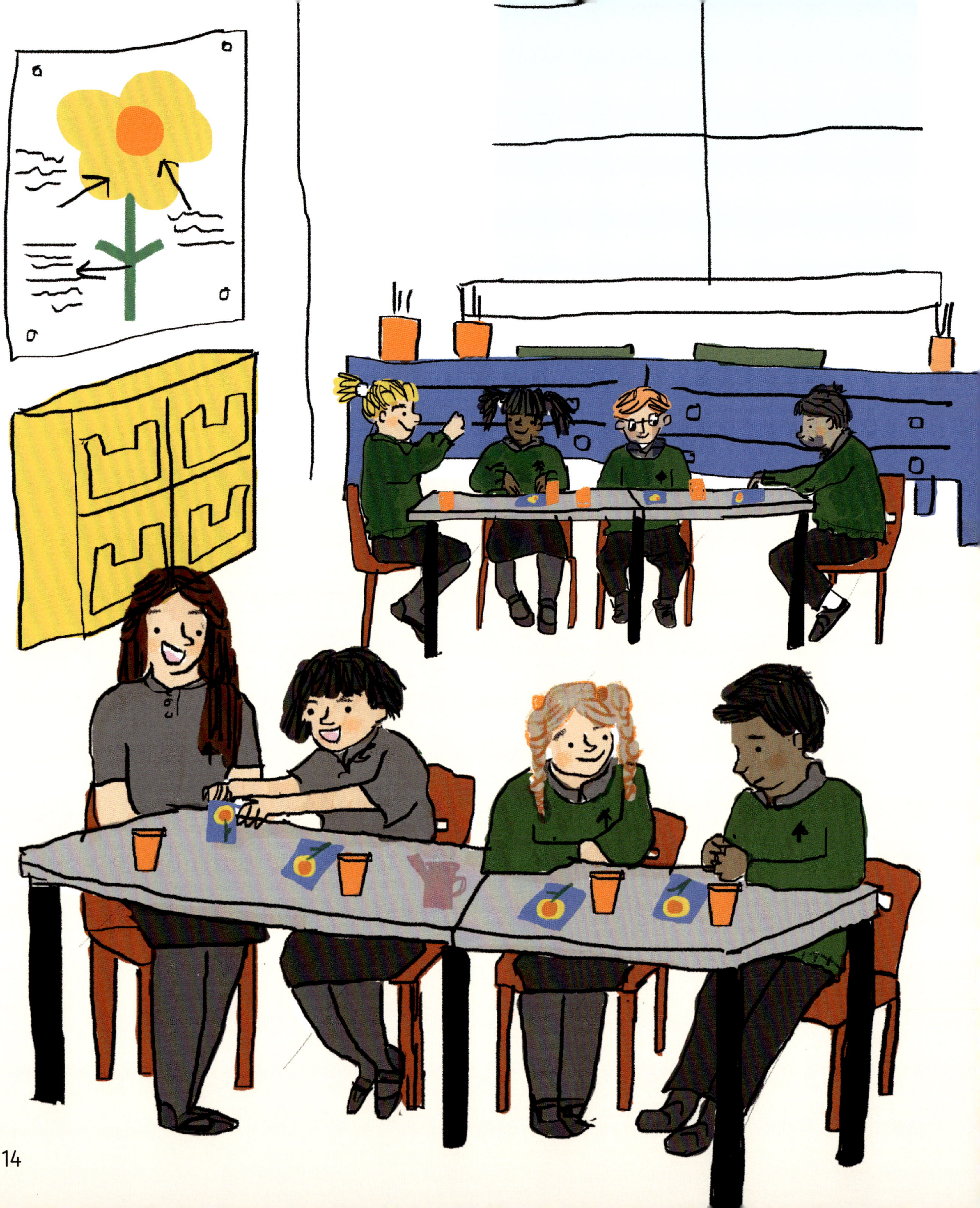

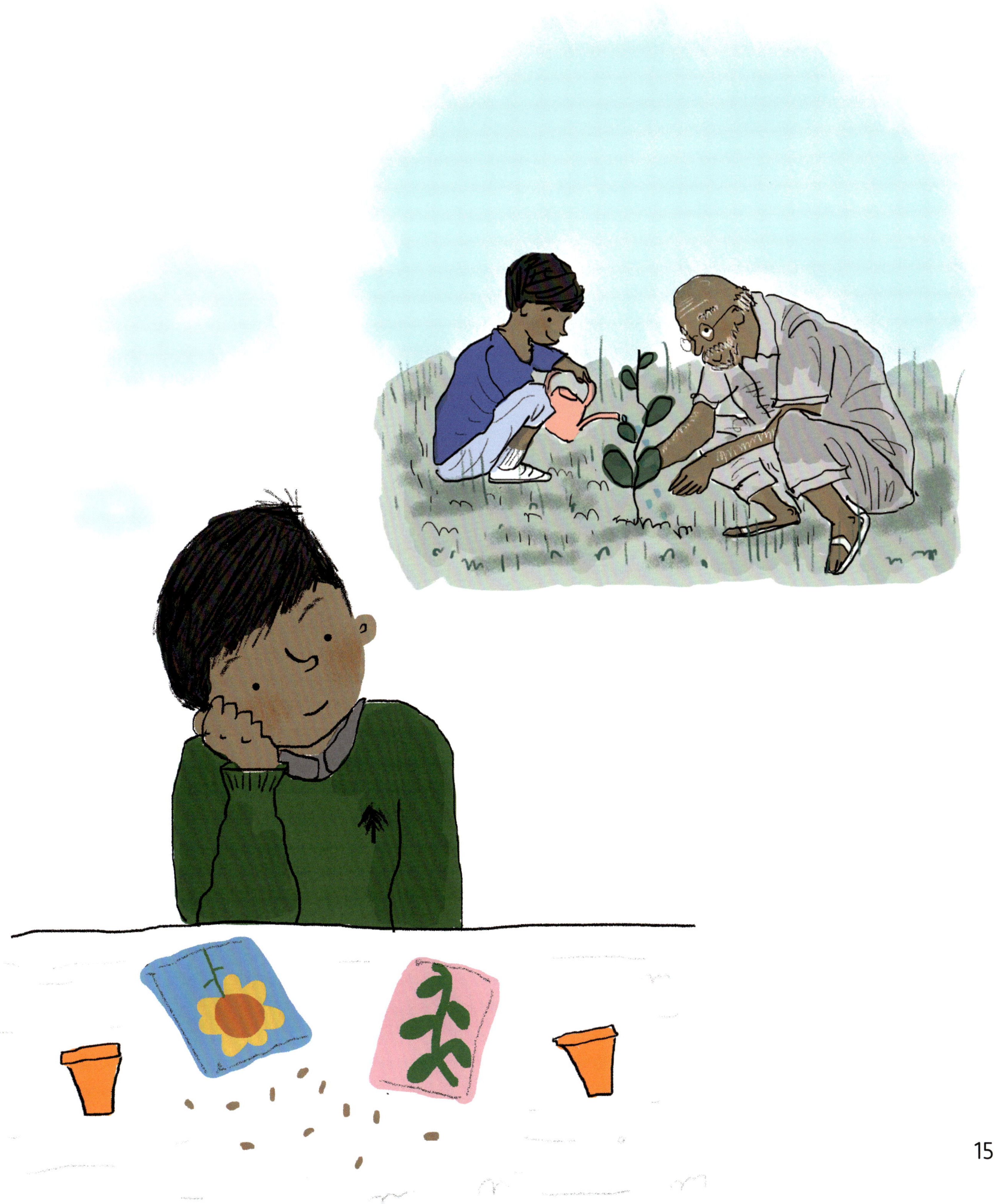

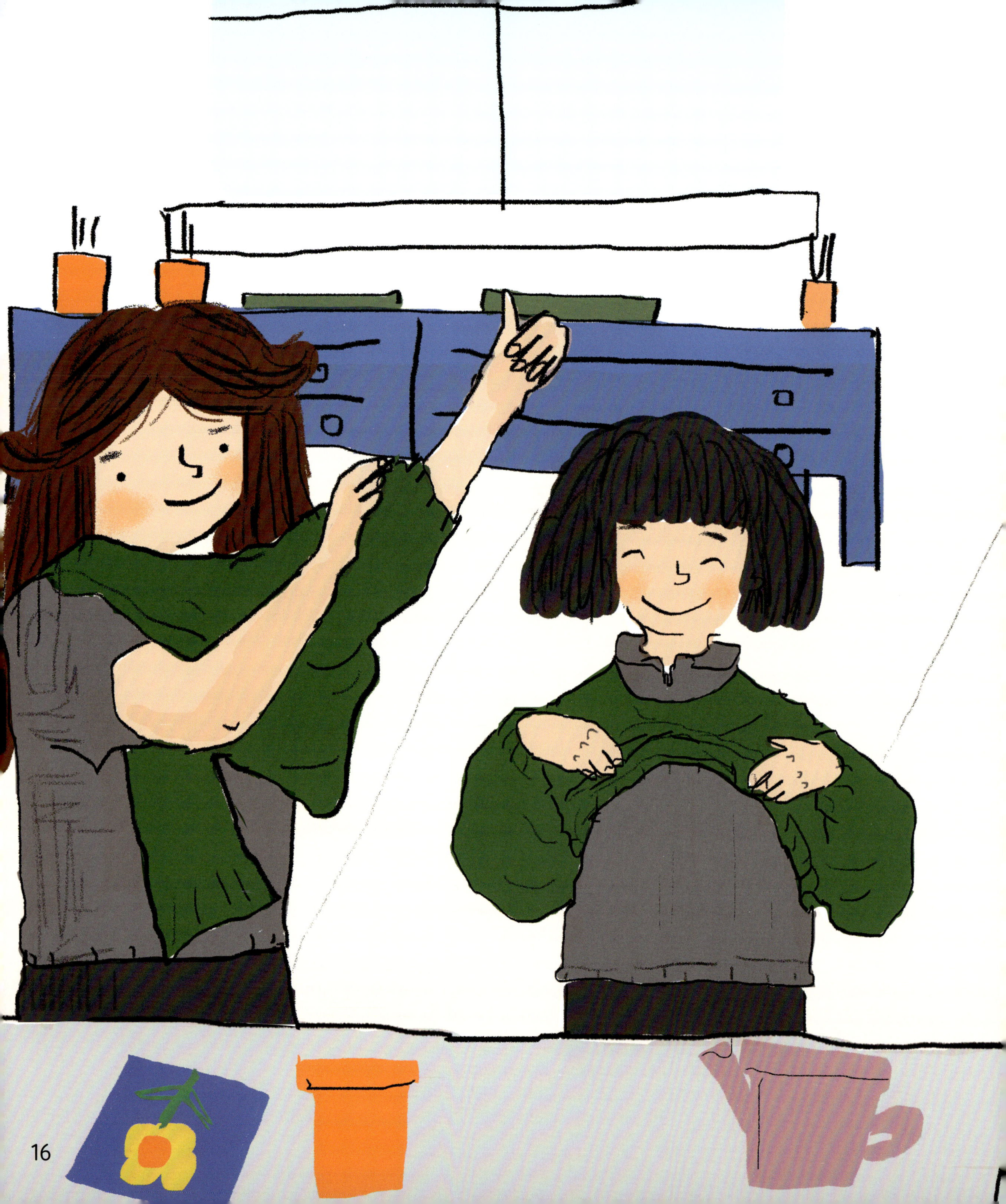

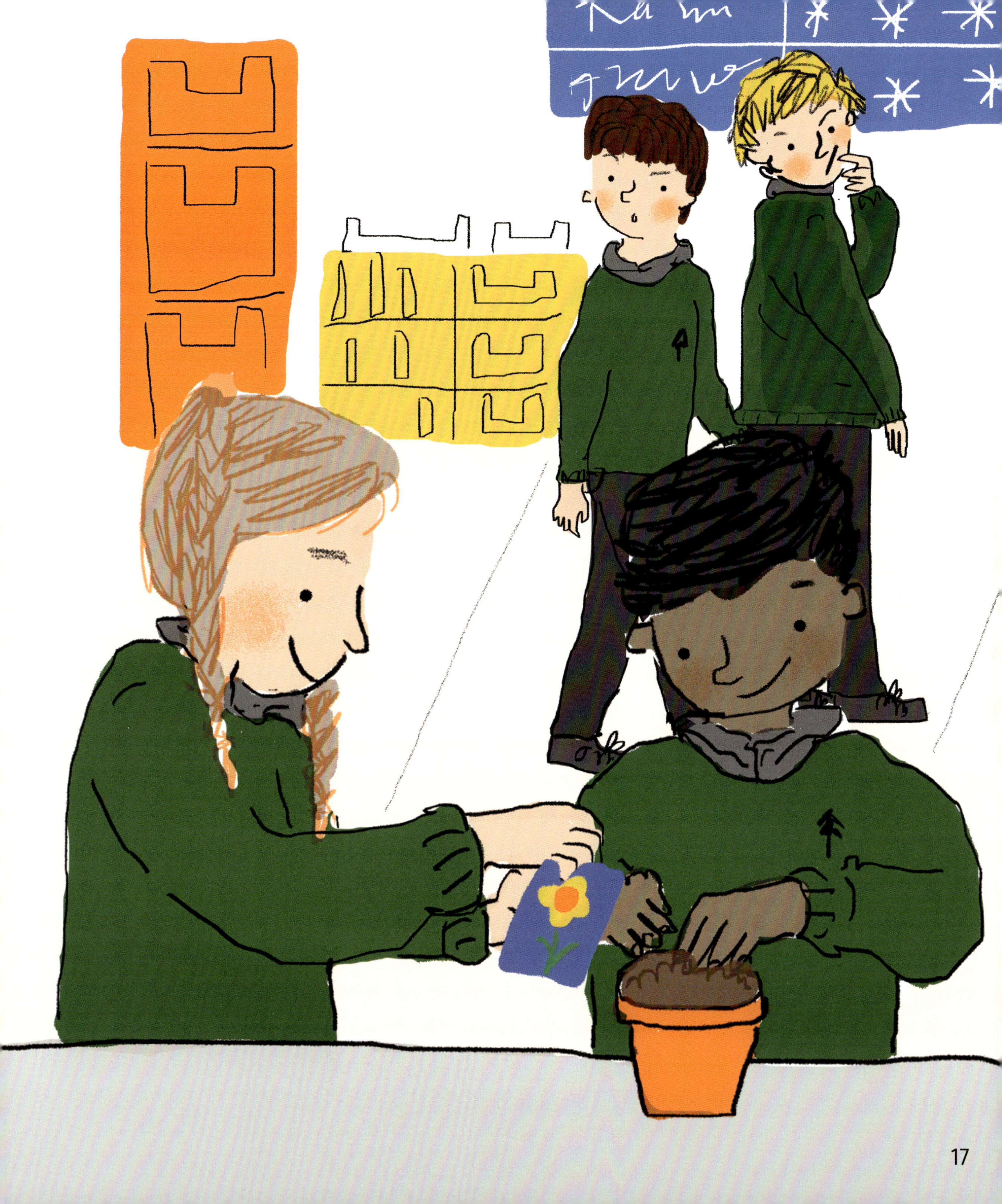

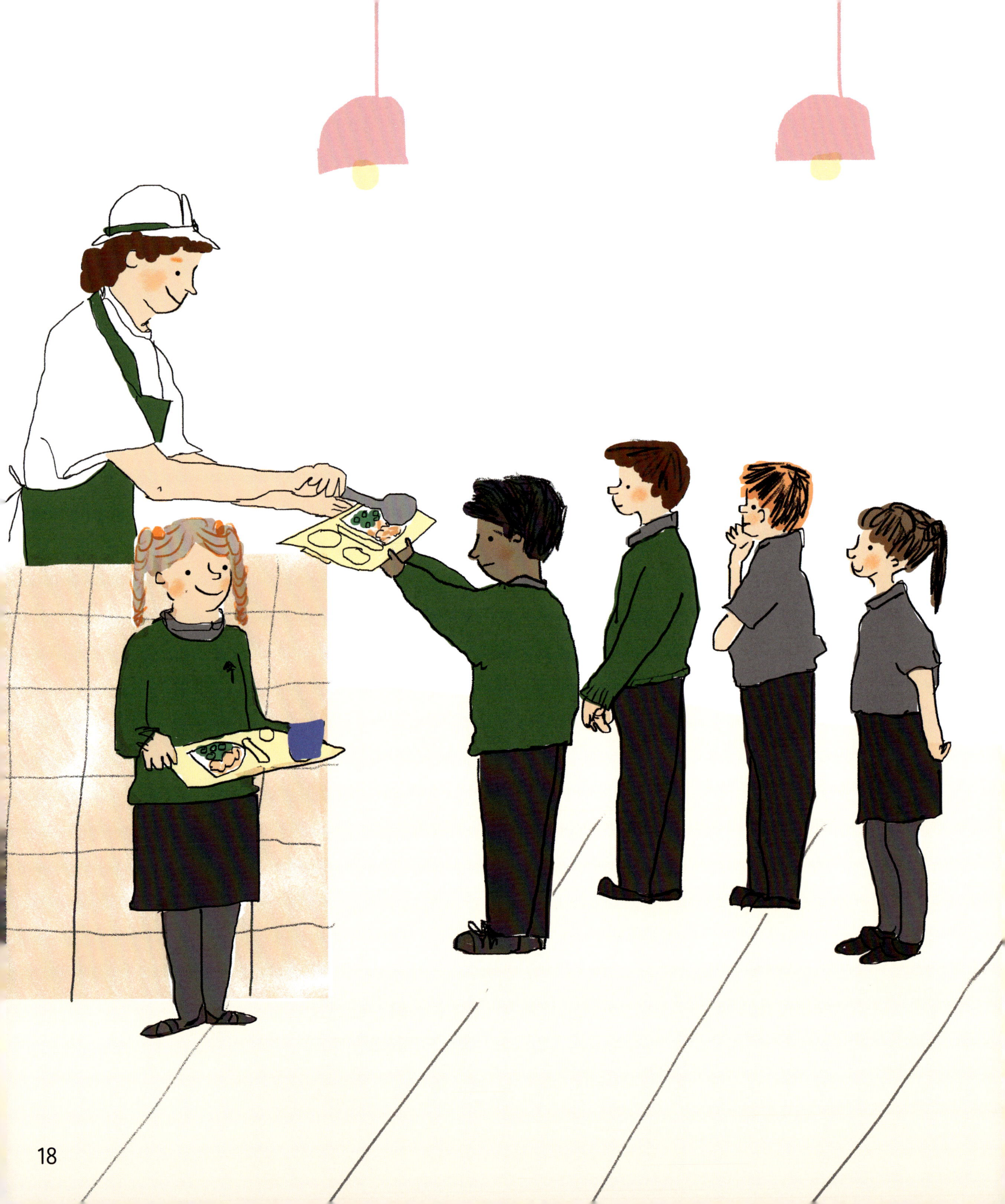

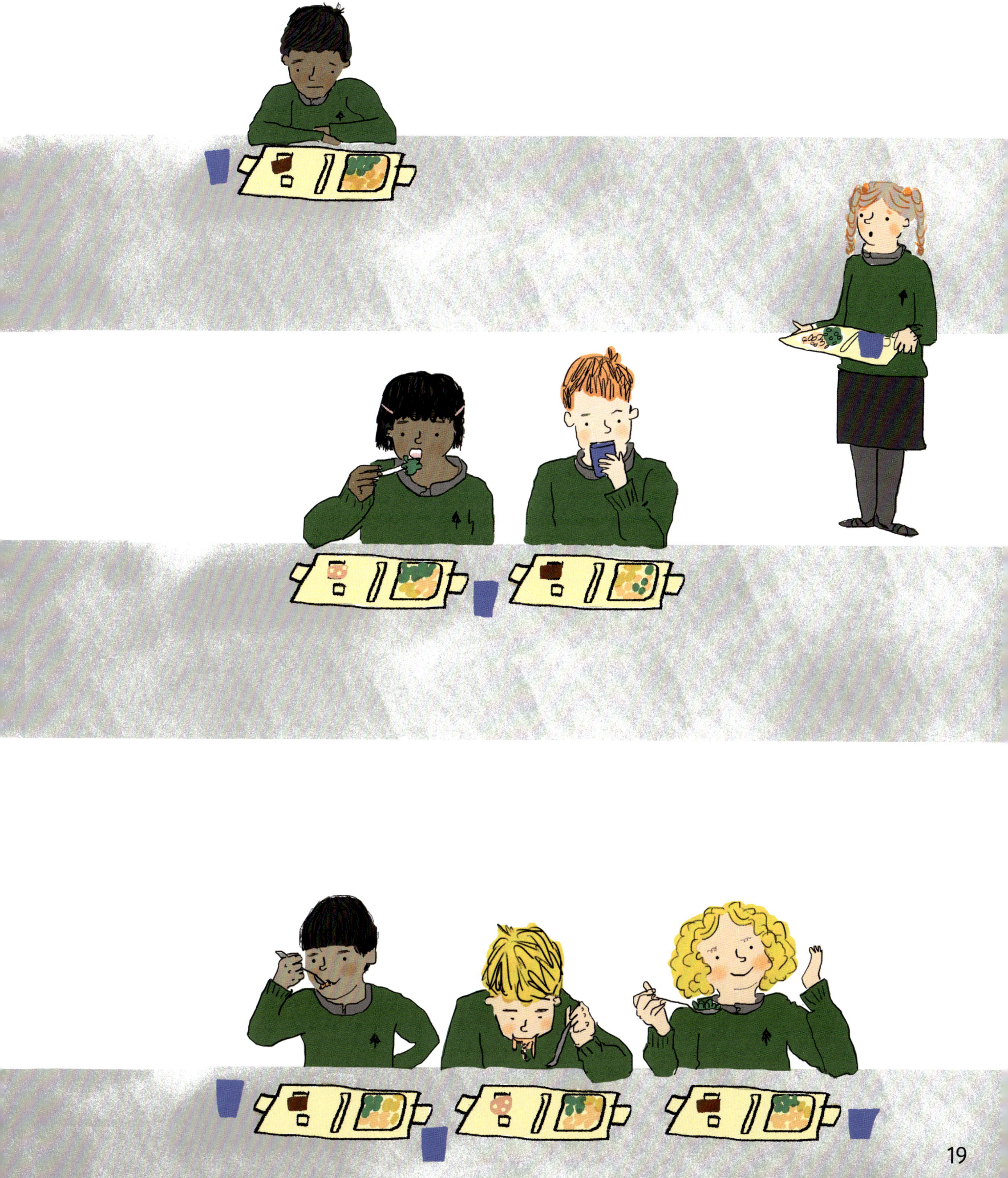

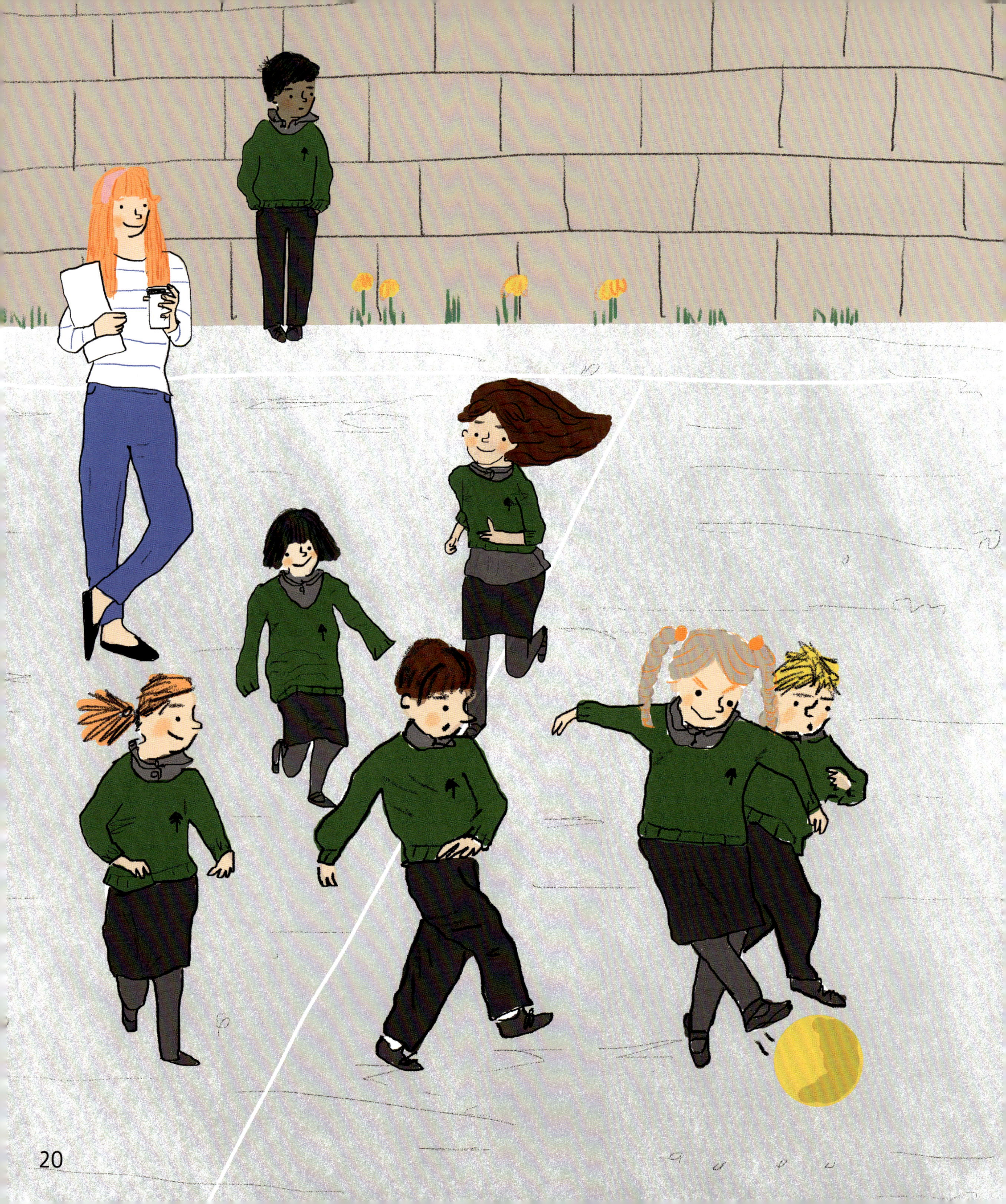

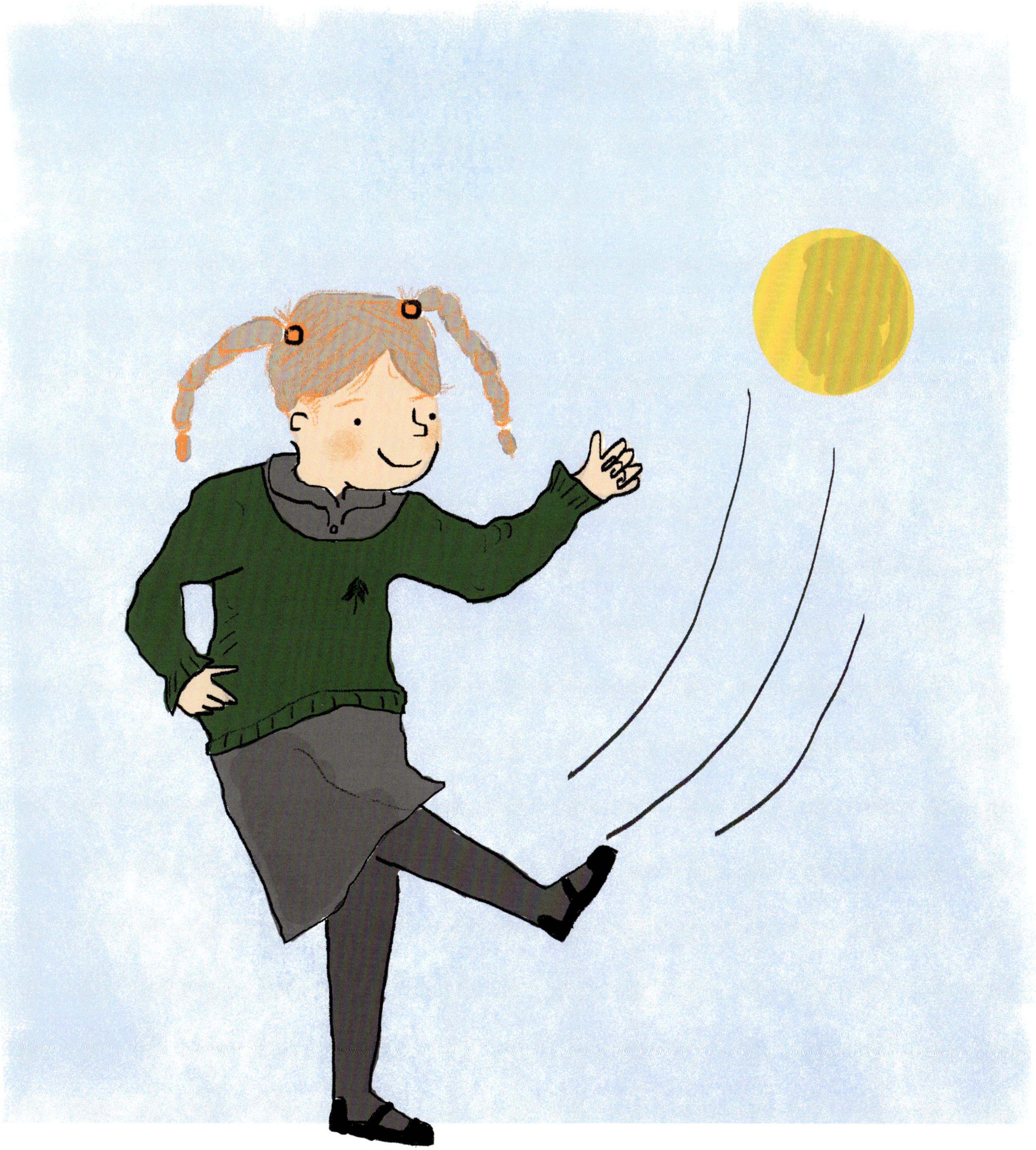

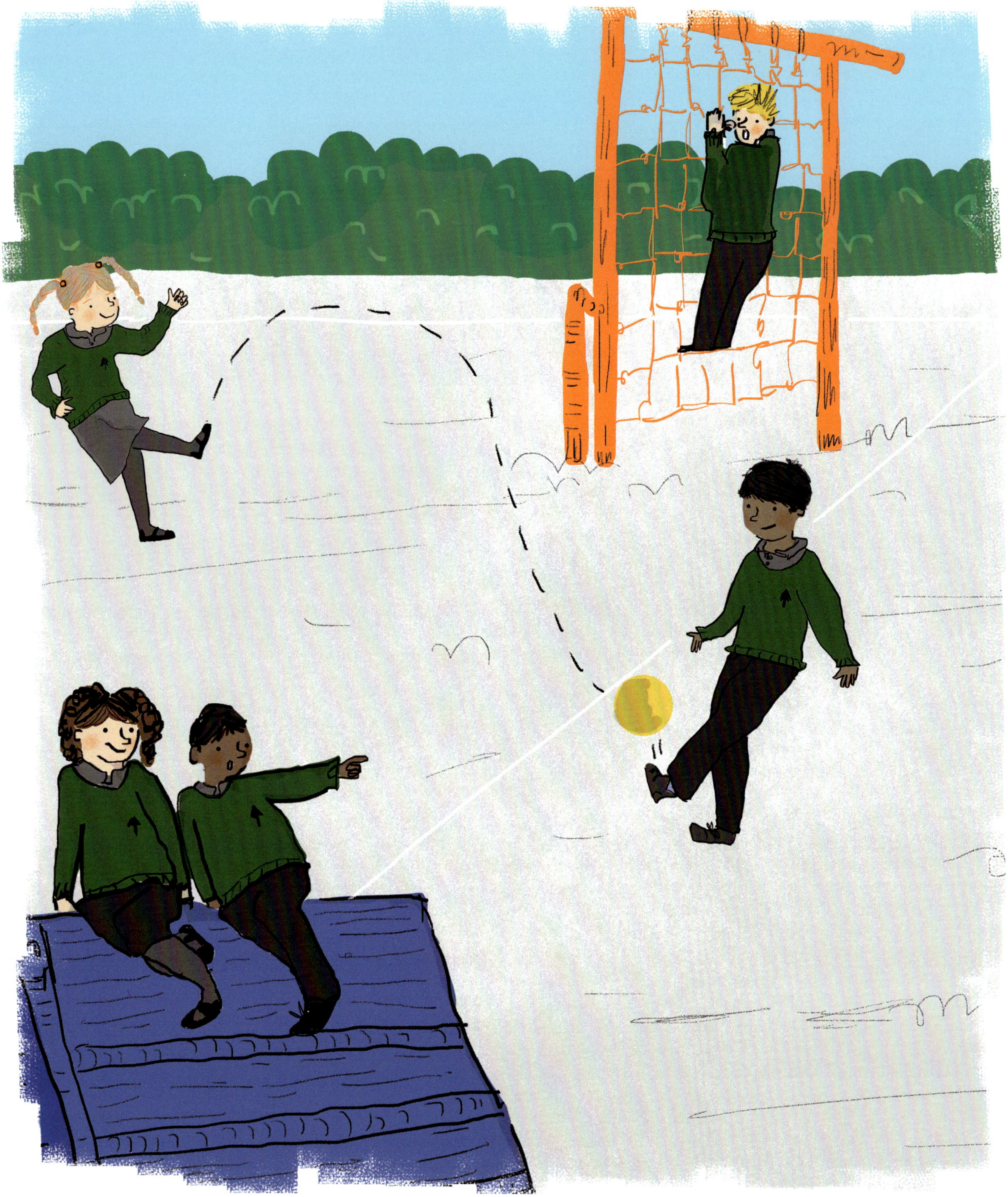

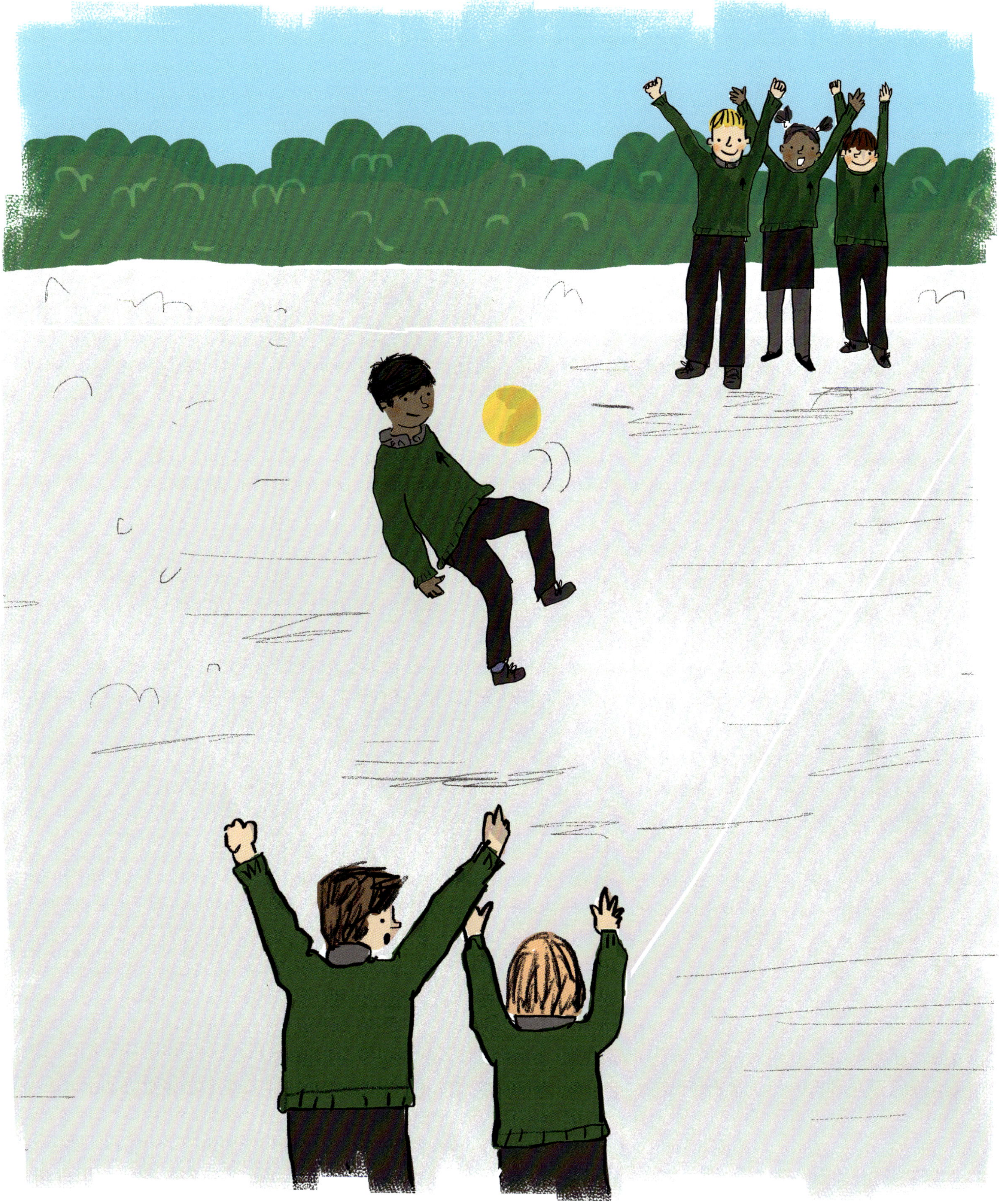

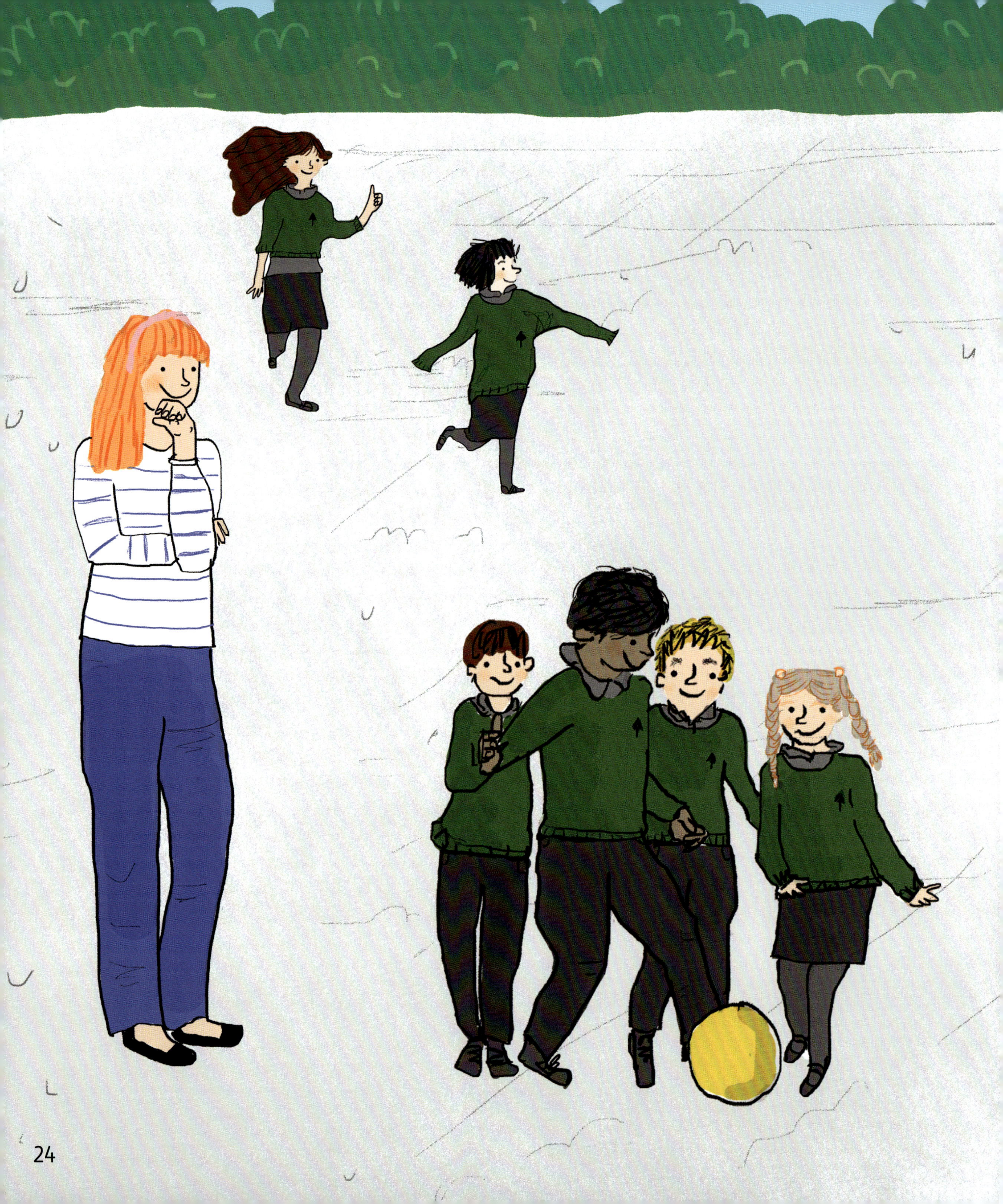

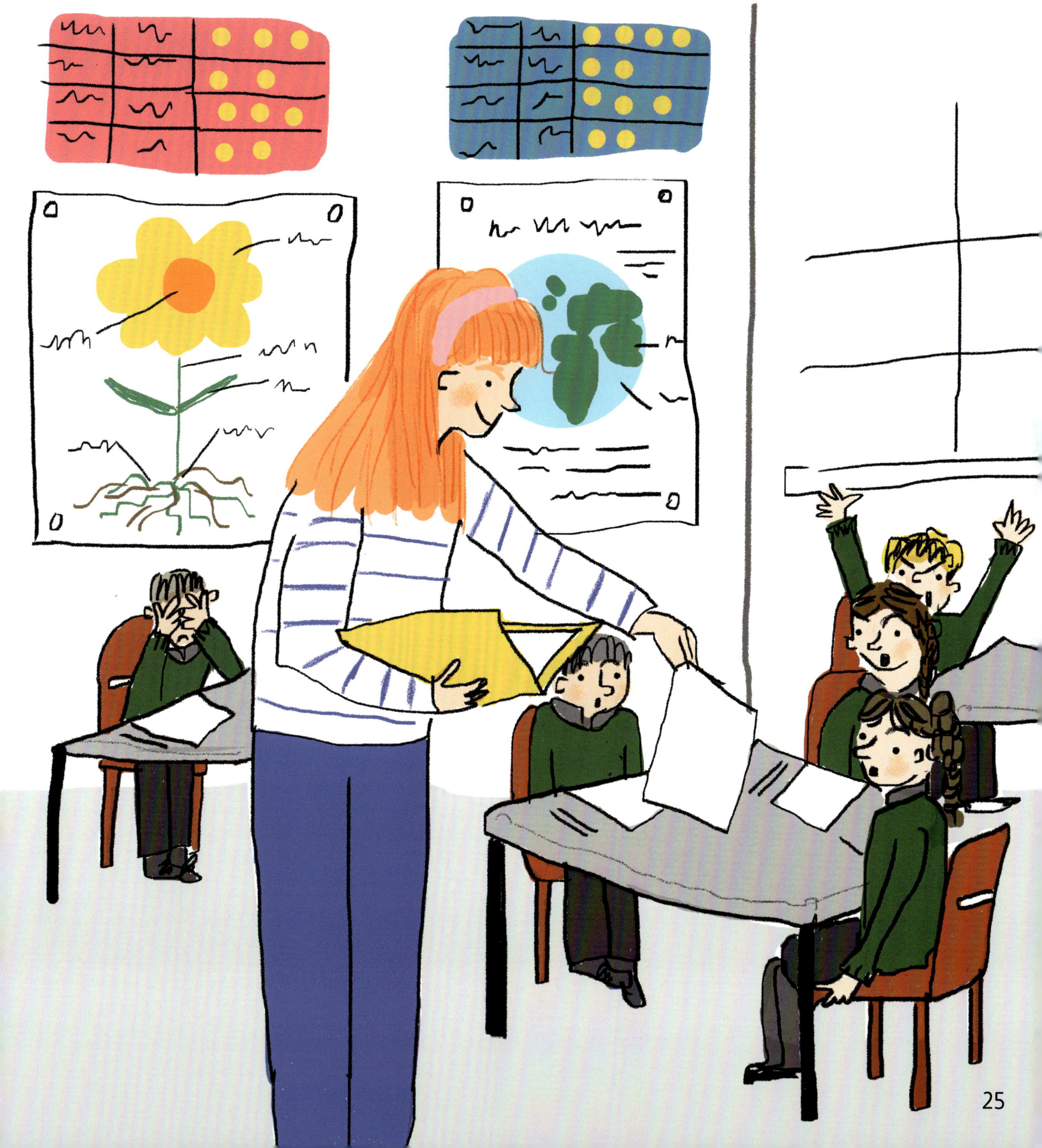

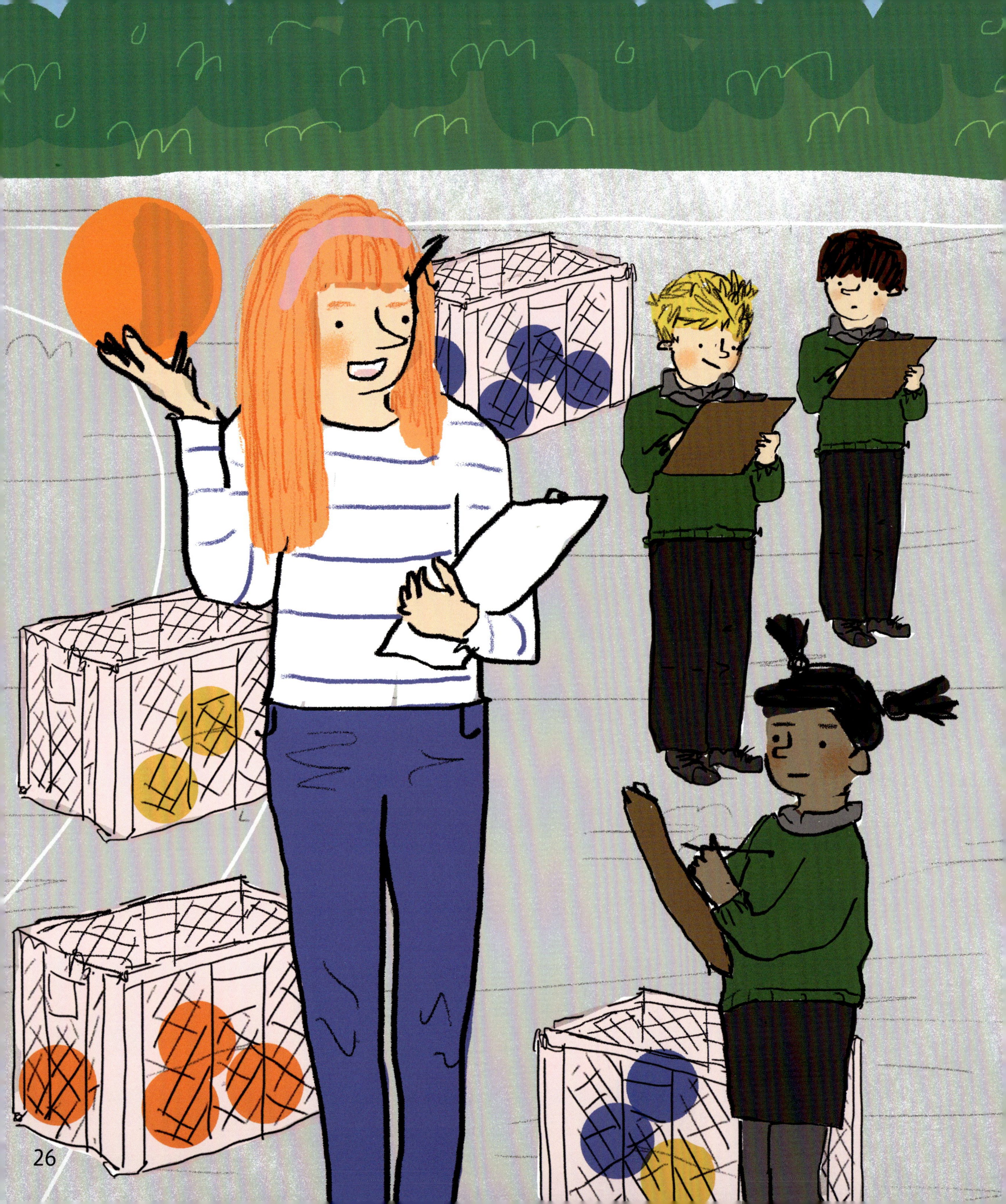

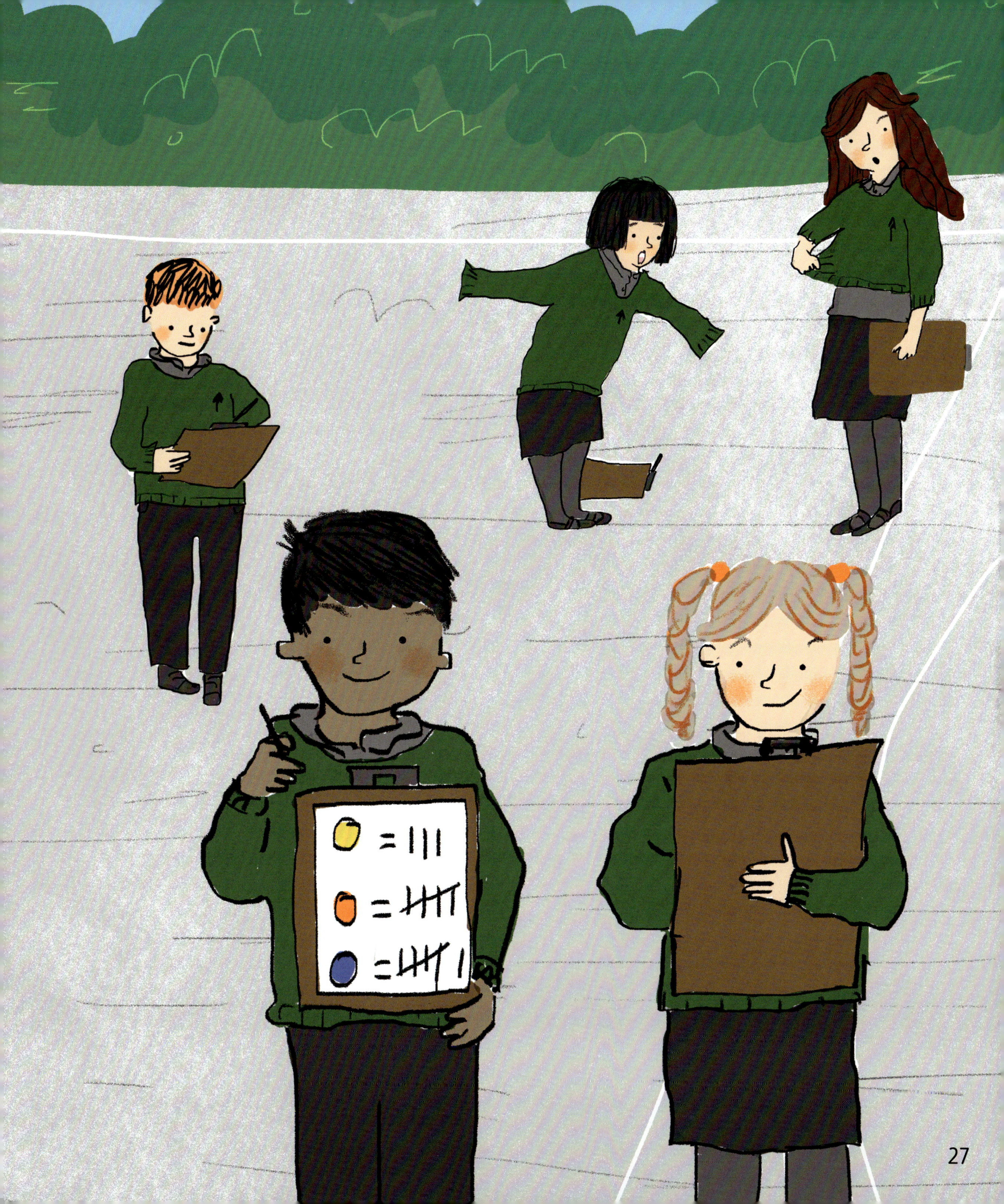
= III
= 卌
= 卌 I

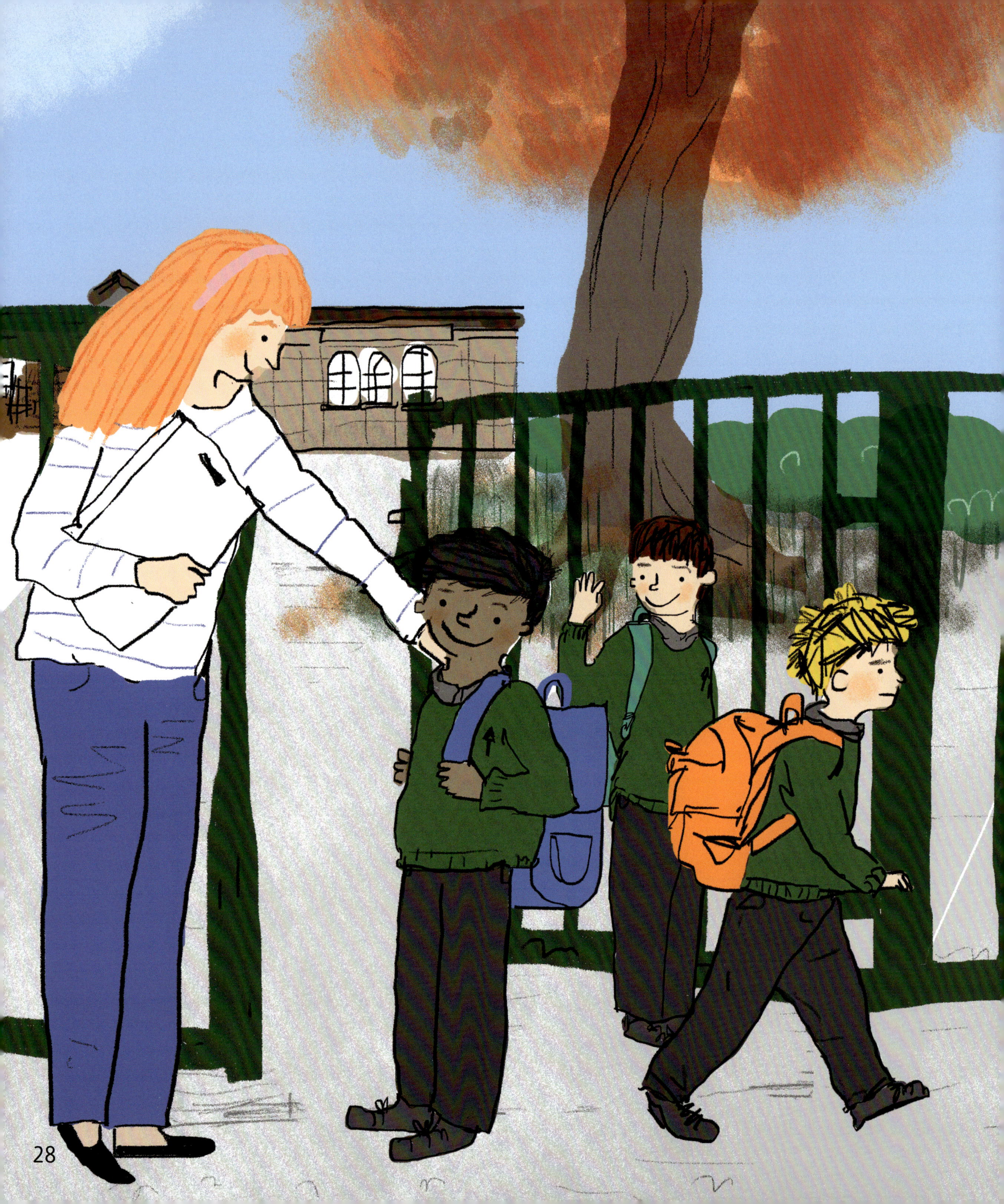

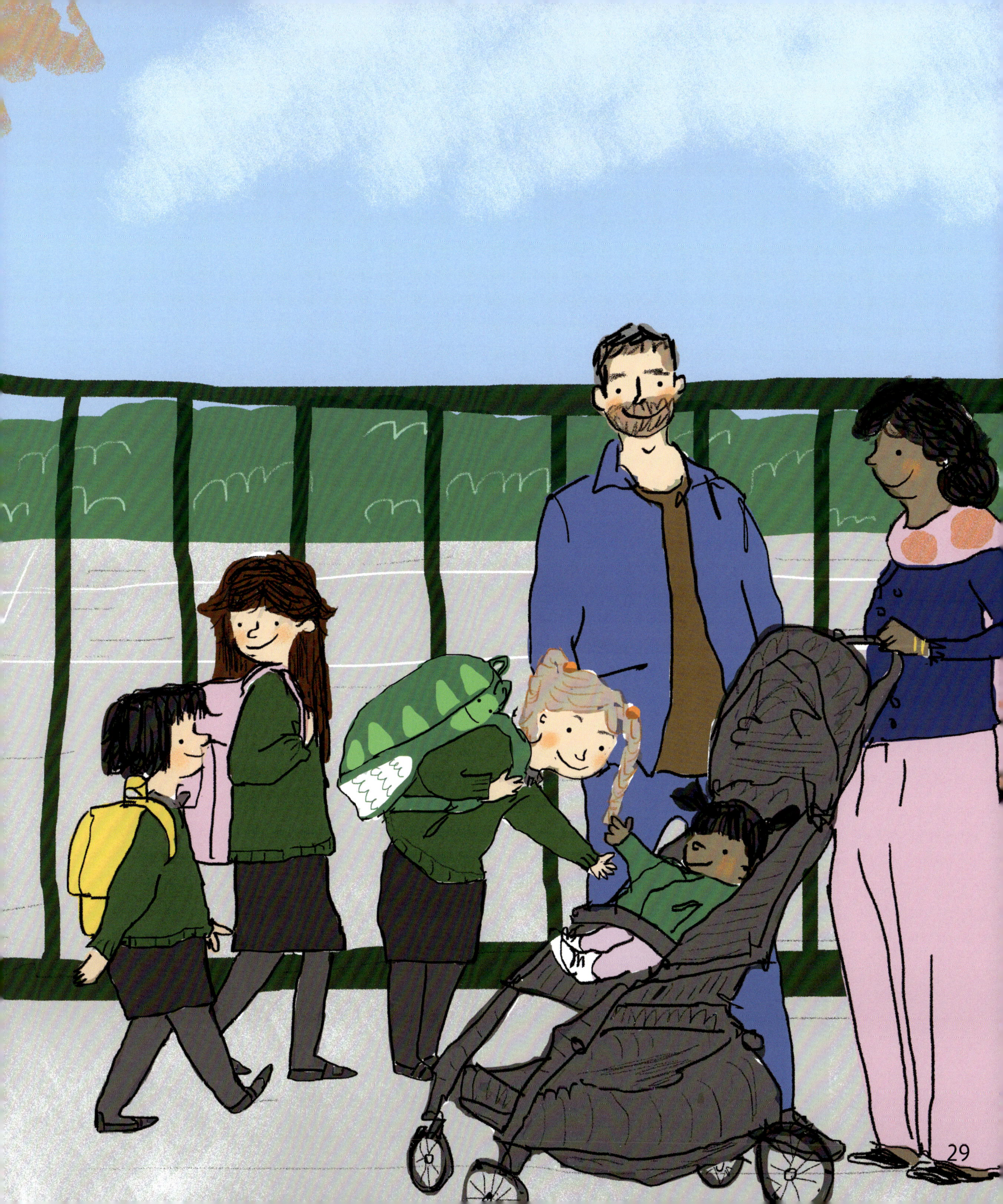

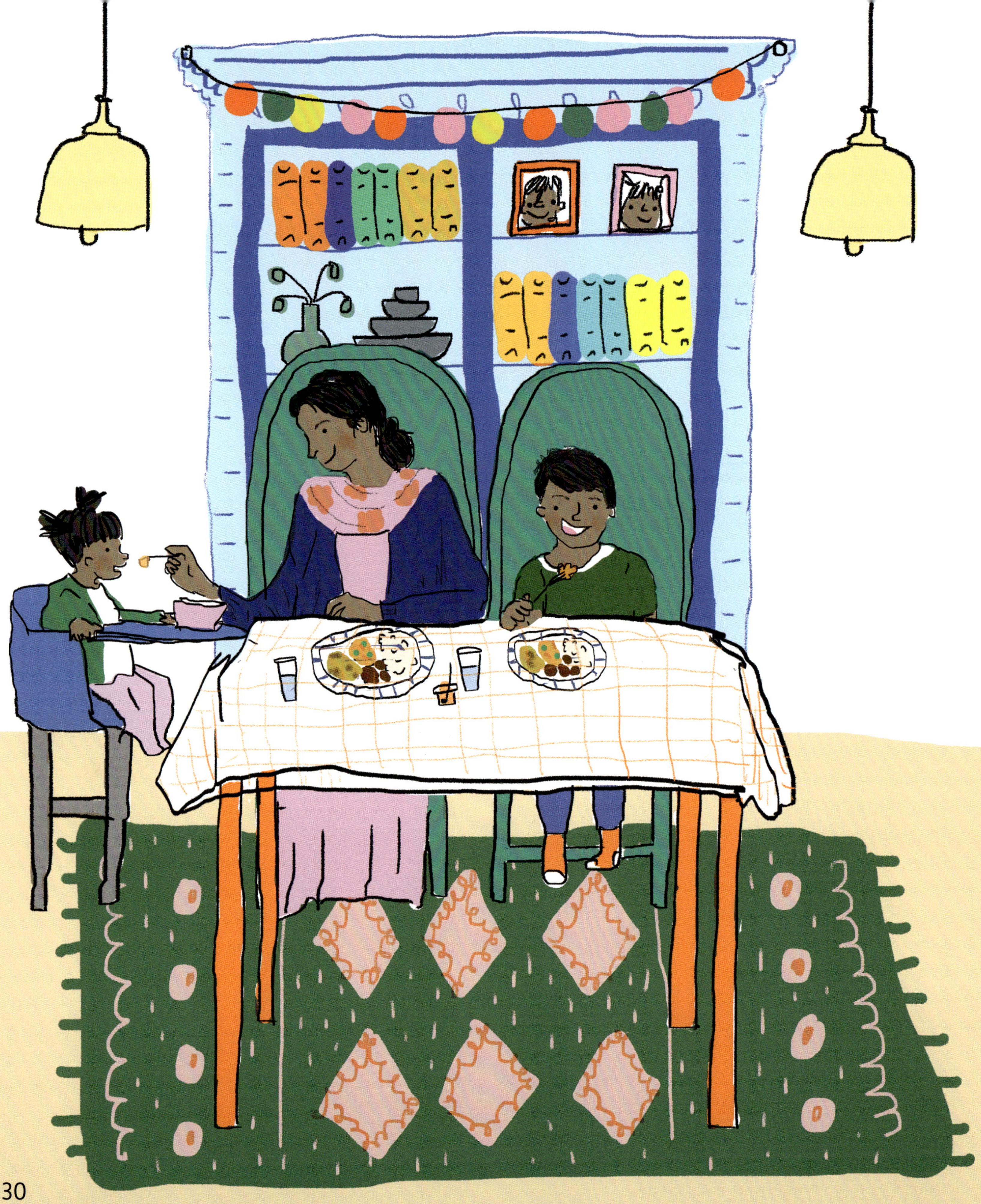

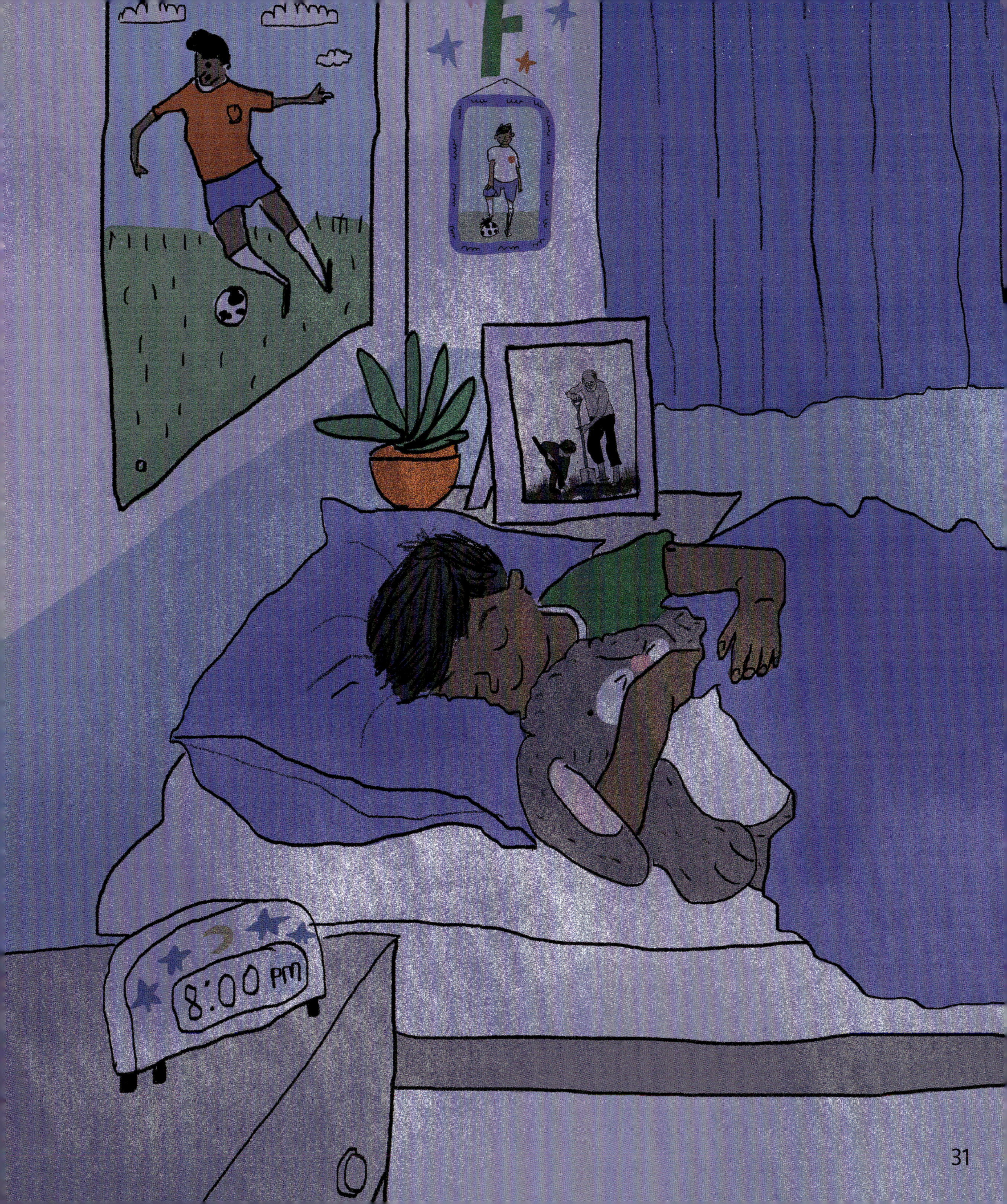
8:00 pm

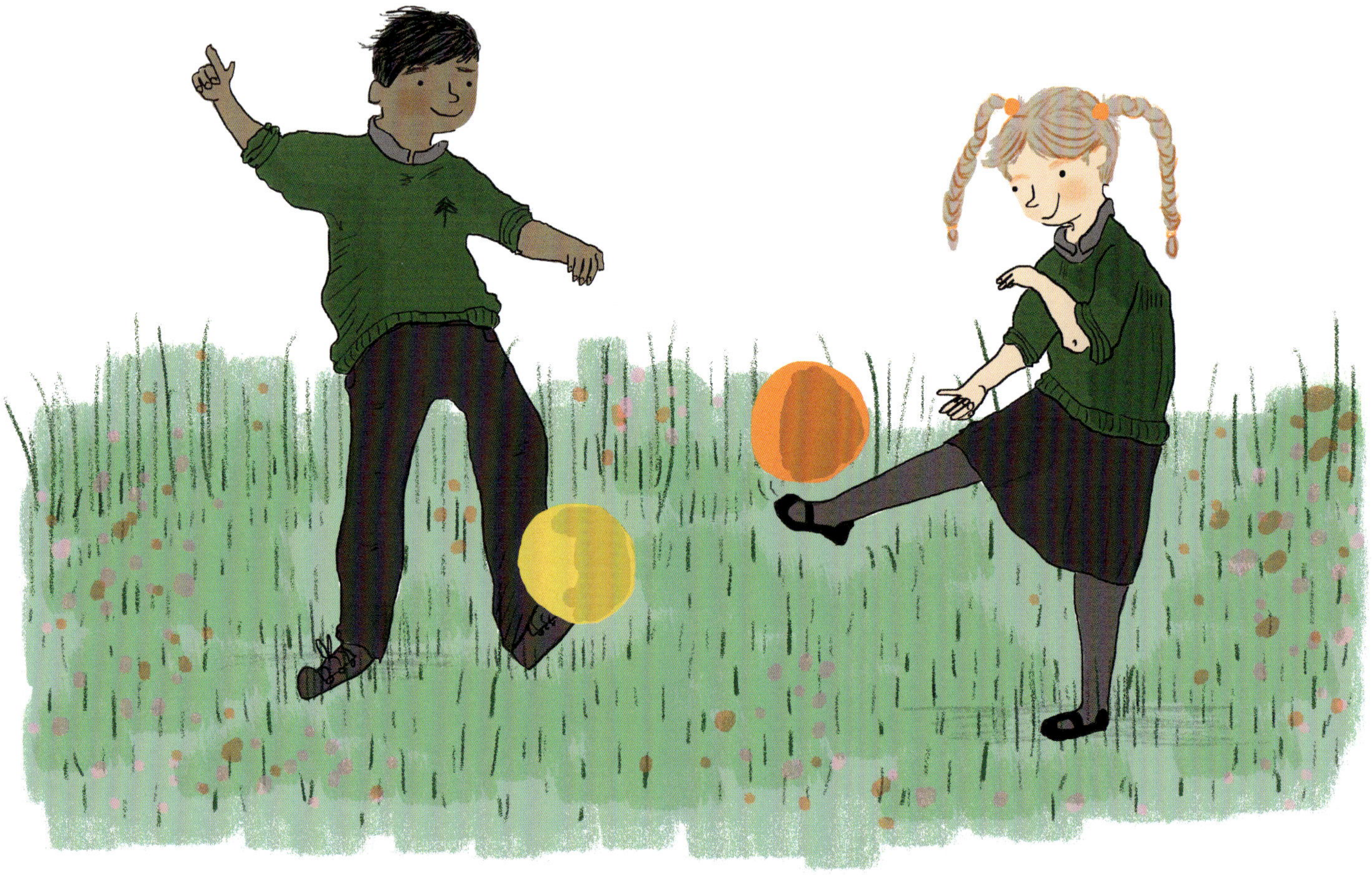